Groups in Social Work

A Workbook

Groups in Social Work

A Workbook

Jacqueline Corcoran
Virginia Commonwealth University

Boston   New York   San Francisco
Mexico City   Montreal   Toronto   London   Madrid   Munich   Paris
Hong Kong   Singapore   Tokyo   Cape Town   Sydney

Senior Acquisitions Editor: Patricia Quinlin
Editorial Assistant: Carly Czech
Senior Marketing Manager: Wendy Albert
Production Assistant: Maggie Brobeck
Manufacturing Buyer: Debbie Rossi
Cover Administrator: Joel Gendron

For related titles and support materials, visit our online catalog at www.pearsonhighered.com.

Between the time website information is gathered and then published, it is not unusual for some sites to have closed. Also, the transcription of URLs can result in unintended typographical errors. The publisher would appreciate notification where these errors occur so that they may be corrected in subsequent editions.

ISBN-13: 978-0-205-54272-7   ISBN-10: 0-205-54272-7

Cataloging-in-Publication data not available at time of publication.

Printed in the United States of America

10 9 8 7 6 5 4 3 2 1   12 11 10 09 08

To my father, Patrick Corcoran

Contents

Acknowledgments

To the students who contributed case vignettes, thank you so much for enlivening this workbook and sharing your learning experiences: Samantha Atkin, Erin Azar, Christopher Dillon, Gidget Fields, Katherine Kestle, Lori Kopp, Wendy Miessler, Nga Nguyen, Margaret Robinson, LeAnn Smuthkochorn, Corey Thornton, and Zoe Rizzuto.

I would also like to thank the reviewers of this text: Thomas A. Artlet, University of Georgia, Athens; Robert Blundo, University of North Carolina, Wilmington; Cheryl K. Brandsen, Calvin College; J. Camille Hall, University of Tennessee; Dina M. Kassler, University of Texas, Austin; Brett Seabury, University of Michigan, Ann Arbor; and Diane R. Weiner, Binghamton University.

Groups in Social Work

A Workbook

Chapter 1
Introduction and Overview

Groups in Social Work: A Workbook will provide social work students and professionals with information on how to lead psychosocial groups, which are defined as interventions directed at a group of individuals to achieve a common goal, with the group being the agent of change. As you probably already know, social work is concerned with the operation of *systems* and how individuals are embedded within systems. Groups are a tangible type of system. Like all systems, they are more than the sum of their parts; they arise out of the interactional patterns among the people in the group, and they seek to establish a homeostasis that is comfortable to the members. You will notice, even in your classes, that the group comprising the class takes on a life or a complexion of its own, which differs from other classes you take. This complexion is a function of the leader (the instructor), the class members, and environmental factors, such as whether the class is offered in a perpetually cold room, at the end of a long day of classes, or whether the program as a whole is run in an organized way, taking students' needs into account.

My rationale for writing this book arises from several avenues. First, group is a primary modality of intervention in the field of social work and in other helping professions. For instance, groups are *the* modality in hospital-based programs (acute psychiatric, day treatment) and in residential treatment. They are also a primary modality of intervention for certain problems (e.g., domestic violence perpetration, substance use disorders) in outpatient treatment. Because social workers will be expected to plan and implement groups in a variety of settings in which they work, it is of vital importance that they be skilled in this modality. Second, social work group facilitators today face certain challenges. They often work with clients who have been mandated to attend groups and those in which membership continually revolves. Further, due to the commitment of social work to oppressed and vulnerable groups, we often work with financially disadvantaged clients and those who face disability, or are from a sexual or ethnic minority group. Focus on these particular challenges is not always captured in other group texts, which may center on largely middle-class clients who are seen in closed-ended, long-term groups (e.g., Corey et al., 1992; Yalom, 2005). You will note in the practice vignettes threaded throughout this text that the majority of examples comprise group participants from socially diverse groups.

Third, years of experience in practice and in teaching have shown me that social workers face some common problems when doing group work; awareness of these potential issues can help with the effective planning and implementation of group services. The approach I will therefore take in *Groups in Social Work* is to provide information rich with examples, as well as practice vignettes so that students learn how to problem solve about group work.

Fourth, students who have not yet had much experience with groups are understandably nervous about acting in a leadership role. Generally, students worry about not knowing what they're doing and about being challenged about their leadership skills. They are anxious about not knowing the answers, looking silly, or being exposed as "an imposter" by the group. The purpose of this workbook will be to help the student feel prepared through imparting basic information on how to lead groups in social work practice. Students will not only take in material, they will be asked to apply their developing knowledge and skills through exercises. Many of the examples and exercises will contain "challenging group moments" that the author and other group leaders have experienced. This workbook will discuss how to prevent difficult situations by making appropriate planning decisions at the outset. At the same time, the nature of groups is that unpredictable situations will arise. Readers will therefore be given the tools to know what to do in such situations and will be more capable of helping participants benefit in the many ways that group intervention can offer.

Fifth, this book was written to encapsulate mandates from the social work profession. The Council on Social Work Education, the institutional body that accredits schools of social work, has in its policy statement several directives. One is that interventions taught in schools of social work should emphasize the "strengths, capacities, and resources of client systems..." (Council on Social Work Education, 2004, p. 4). The client systems that will be emphasized in this book will primarily be groups and individuals as members of groups. *Groups in Social Work* will take a strengths-based orientation toward groups. A strengths-based orientation is respectful of the individual, one of social work's prime values, in that it recognizes people's capacities and focuses on the development of environmental supports rather than taking a pathological view of the individual. People who are empowered are more motivated to engage in intervention and are more inspired to make changes.

In *Groups in Social Work*, solution-focused therapy and motivational interviewing will be used to ensure that a strengths-based orientation is maintained. We will briefly describe these models here. Developed by de Shazer, Berg, and colleagues (Berg, 1994; Berg & Miller, 1992; Cade & O'Hanlon, 1993; De Jong, Berg, Kleiner, & Mamiya, 2008; De Shazer, Berg, Lipchick, Nunnally, Molnar, Gingerich, & Weiner-Davis, 1986; O'Hanlon & Weiner-Davis, 1989), solution-focused therapy emphasizes client strengths, abilities, and resources (Marsden, 1995; O'Hanlon & Weiner-Davis, 1989). Clients are assumed to have the necessary resources to solve their own problems through resources that are found by eliciting and exploring times when the problem does not exert its negative influence and/or when the client has coped successfully. The assumption in solution-focused therapy is that change occurs in a systemic way. Small change is all that is necessary as a "spiral effect" takes place: the client takes a step in the right direction; others in the context respond differently; the client feels more empowered and is encouraged toward further change. Both behaving differently and thinking differently are part of the processes of change (De Shazer, 1994).

Since no one holds the objective truth, individuals are valued for their unique perspective with the right to determine their own goals. Clients are encouraged to find the solutions that fit their own worldview. The practitioner works collaboratively with the client to build client awareness of strengths. These strengths are then mobilized and applied to problem situations.

Motivational interviewing is "a client-centered, directive method for enhancing intrinsic motivation to change by exploring and resolving ambivalence" (Miller & Rollnick, 2002, p. 25). Motivational interviewing is generally used when people have not yet decided whether they want to change. For this reason, motivational interviewing techniques might be especially helpful for people who have been mandated to attend treatment, as most are not convinced they should make a change. Several guiding principles underlie the techniques of motivational interviewing. These include expressing empathy, developing discrepancy between problem behaviors and the clients' goals and values, rolling with resistance rather than confronting it, supporting and enhancing self-efficacy, and developing a change plan.

Techniques from solution-focused therapy and motivational interviewing will be integrated throughout the book, and Chapter 11 will be devoted to strengths-based techniques that are not covered elsewhere. Both solution-focused therapy and motivational interviewing offer ways to ensure that the group leader works collaboratively with clients, even when they are mandated to attend treatment. Because of social work's traditional commitment to oppressed and vulnerable populations, it means that social workers will often be involved in leading groups with such populations, who have not chosen to be part of formal intervention. These group members deserve a collaborative approach that conveys the message that, ultimately, they are the experts on their lives.

Another emphasis by the Council on Social Work Education is that social work practitioners must show competence in identifying, analyzing, and applying empirically based interventions following the recent movement in the helping and social science professions towards *evidence-based practice*. Evidence-based practice means that social workers choose interventions based on the extent to which research evidence supports their use. In this book, an evidence-based approach will be exemplified in two chief ways: through the choice of empirically tested curricula and through the promotion of evaluation tools to assess the progress of the individual members in group.

To summarize, *Groups in Social Work: A Workbook* will offer the following:

- Practical, jargon-free information on planning and implementing group services with plenty of opportunities to practice skills and knowledge in practice vignettes. Answers are provided in an instructor's manual.

- An abundance of examples from diverse practice settings (medical hospitals, psychiatric hospitals, residential treatment programs, schools, clubhouse settings, substance use treatment programs, child protective services) and types of groups (support, psychoeducational, and treatment groups), which will be threaded throughout the workbook.

- How to locate group curricula and the provision of an appendix of curricula and manuals that have been gathered for different problems for which people might seek group intervention.

- How to work with non-voluntary group members.

- How to evaluate the effectiveness of groups.

- Maintaining a strengths-based focus.

ADVANTAGES AND DISADVANTAGES OF GROUP WORK

Question 1.1: What do you consider some of the benefits of group interventions for the people that participate in them? List these here before you read ahead.

Advantages

There are many advantages for people attending groups, as identified by Yalom (2005). First, people realize, from being part of a group, the *universality of experience*. They see they are not the only ones suffering from a particular problem. In a broader sense, they see they are not alone struggling with existential issues of humanity, such as recognizing that life is at times unfair, acknowledging that we will all die eventually, finding meaning, and realizing that regardless of how much help we receive from others, we alone are responsible for the way we live our lives.

Along with universalizing, *normalizing* also occurs. People understand that they are not different or "crazy" because they experience difficulty with a particular problem. They see that others are similarly afflicted, which, on its own, often allays people's concerns and fears to a great degree. Normalizing also involves educating people about the reactions and concerns people often experience when they encounter a certain problem. For example, crime victims, cancer patients, caregivers of the elderly, and sexual abuse victims need information about the problem and its particular dynamics in order to understand their reactions and what they can expect in the recovery process.

An additional advantage of group attendance is that people are provided with hope, the belief that it is possible for their lives to change and have different outcomes. When members are able to gain hope, they begin to perceive that they are not powerless over their lives, and that they do have choices. "Hope is therapeutic in itself, for it gives members the confidence to commit themselves to the demanding work that a group requires and motivates them to explore alternatives" (Corey, 2008, p. 99). Hope is provided when people see that others have changed as a result of attending group. It also sometimes comes after a person has been challenged by other group members to entertain alternative views and outlooks than the ones they have held onto in the past.

Yet another powerful process of groups is that they become a social microcosm for participants. That is, members interact in the patterned way they relate to others in their lives. With the facilitator's assistance, people can learn about their interpersonal functioning, obtain a more accurate view of how they are perceived, and practice new ways of relating, which can be carried over into the person's social environment. As Yalom (1985) acknowledges, "It is extremely difficult to try out new behavior in one's ordinary social surroundings. The risks are high: valuable relationships may be fractured; people upon whom one is dependent may go away; one has no assurance of receiving honest...responses from others" (p. 176). In the group setting, one can experiment with new ways of relating, and these behaviors may then translate into contexts outside the group.

An additional advantage of groups is that they replicate childhood patterns, with the leader seen as "the parent," and the other group members as "siblings" who compete for parental attention. This dynamic is intensified in the presence of a male-female team of co-leaders. If members are able to process these reactions in the group situation and are heard and validated, and if they see the group leader is concerned about them and the others in the group, they can achieve some healing around their earlier experiences.

There are many other benefits to groups. People gain self-knowledge as they interact with each other and get feedback. They experience catharsis as they express emotions and are accepted by others. They further observe the treatment of other members with similar problems and apply members' insights to their own lives. Members also experience a sense of altruism when they help others through sharing insights, feedback, and support. Further, group members learn social skills, such as speaking authentically about the self, listening and validating others, and asking for what one needs.

One more inherent advantage of groups is that members can rely on each other to maintain their commitment to change either in the group or by contacting each other outside of group time if they should need additional support (Corey, 2008). This is one reason Alcoholics Anonymous has worked so well for many people with addictions. Members struggling with urges to use can call their sponsors or anyone else in the group, as phone numbers are routinely provided.

Finally, people can take feedback from their peers—people whom they see as similar to themselves with some of the same experiences—that they are unable to hear from therapists and other authority figures in groups (Toseland & Rivas, 2009).

Question 1.2: What do you see as the disadvantages of groups? List them here before reading ahead.

Disadvantages

Although certain disadvantages will be named below, if the group leader is aware of these possible problems, they often can be avoided or managed (Rose, 2004). First, people are often reluctant to attend groups. The potential advantages of group (detailed previously) need to be explained to potential members. Second, logistical issues are often involved in getting members together at the same time to hold a group. These issues include scheduling, transportation to groups, and childcare. Third, maintaining confidentially in groups can be difficult as group members do not have professional training and might not see its necessity (Rose, 2004). Fourth, some people need more individual attention than they can receive in group. For instance, if a person is suicidal, he or she would not typically be placed into group. However, people often attend both group and individual treatment as their needs exceed what they would receive in group treatment alone. Fifth, in groups with non-voluntary populations, members may learn and have antisocial behaviors reinforced (Rooney & Chovanec, 2004). Sixth, groups can be subject to "group think" in which individual needs, opinions, and experiences are subjugated to the more dominant group members. Other antitherapeutic norms may develop in group without a skilled leader to deal with them (Rose, 2004). The focus of this workbook will be on the development of your skills so that you will be equipped to lead groups.

ORGANIZATION OF THE BOOK

Groups in Social Work will begin with a description of different types of group interventions. A case will be made for the use of manualized curriculums that already have research support behind them. Considerable time will be spent on how to plan a group so that its chances of success are optimized. We will then cover the stages of group development. The middle stage, or working part of group, will comprise the chapters on strengths-based work, a dominant theme throughout the book, and cognitive-behavioral techniques. After the ending stage, we will go into how to approach challenges to group leadership. The book will end with a chapter on working with diverse groups, continuing a focus on strengths-based work.

Chapter 2
Types of Groups and Group Curricula

In this chapter, I will discuss some interrelated concepts. These include types of groups, the purpose of groups, theoretical orientation, and curricula. All of these must logically relate to the population you are trying to help and the problem you want to impact.

TYPES OF GROUPS

Several typologies of groups have been developed (Reid, 1997; Toseland & Rivas, 2009), but I offer what I see as the most parsimonious way to classify groups and to reflect current practice realities. These are: self-help groups, support groups, educational groups, psychoeducational groups, therapy groups, and task groups. (See Box 2.1 on page 8.) Self-help groups and task groups will not be a focus of this workbook, as the emphasis will remain with psychosocial groups in which professional social work leadership skills are necessary.

Psychosocial groups exist on a continuum in terms of the amount of structure required. "Structure refers to the use of planned, systematic, time-limited interventions and program activities" (Toseland & Rivas, 2009, p. 257). For instance, educational and psychoeducational groups are, by their nature, structured by the information presented. Therapy groups range considerably in the amount of structure used, depending on the following factors:

1. The purpose of the group and its theoretical orientation. (For example: cognitive-behavioral groups tend to be structured in nature, offering information on cognitive-behavioral techniques, the modeling of techniques, role playing, and homework assignments.)

2. Whether the group is open-ended, which means that group membership revolves, and new members enter and existing members leave the group from session to session (discussed further in Chapter 3). In general, open-ended groups require more structure because they cannot progress through the stages of group development in which the therapeutic work may occur. In open-ended groups, members do not get to know each other and become intimate through testing, processing, and working to change their interpersonal functioning as seen in the more mature stages of group development in closed-ended groups. Instead, they have to rely on the structure of the group to help them achieve the purpose of the group.

Box 2.1 Typology of Groups (drawn from Toseland & Rivas, 2009; Corey, 2008; Reid, 1997).

Type of Groups	Emphasis	Examples
Self-help groups	Formed around a common problem that members share--characterized by a peer leader-ship format. Members share experiences, provide emotional and social support, and offer suggestions to one another.	AA, NA, and other 12-step groups
Support groups	To foster mutual aid and to enhance members' coping abilities when members struggle around a common stressful life event. Members recount the stressful life event, ventilate feelings, and discuss efforts to cope.	An HIV/AIDS support group in a health organization serving clients with HIV and AIDS
Educational groups	To help members acquire relevant information and learn new skills. Self-disclosure by members is relatively low as the group is structured around presentation of material, which is seen as more important than the needs of members to self-disclose.	Health education group offered to people with schizophrenia in a club-house setting
Psychoeducational groups	Structured groups that offer educational material on certain problem areas and skills on how to cope with these problems. Along with education, members' emotional and psychological reactions to and experiences with the problem, along with their reactions to the information presented, are processed.	A psychoeducational group for the relatives of people with schizophrenia held at a residential treatment facility
Therapy (or treatment) groups	Help members change their behavior, cope with and ameliorate personal problems or rehabilitate themselves after physical, psychological, or social trauma.	A therapy group for women with depression held at a women's counseling center
Task groups	Groups of professionals that join together to find solutions to organizational problems, generate new ideas, and make decisions. Three main purposes: • meet client needs (teams and staff-development groups) • meet organizational needs (committees, cabinets, and boards of directors) • to meet community needs (social action groups)	Interdisciplinary team that meets in an inpatient psychiatric unit of a hospital to discuss client case plans and progress, as well as administrative issues involved with the smooth running of the unit

3. The duration of the group. If a group is brief in nature (six to eight sessions), there may be a need for more structure so that people can achieve their purposes in coming to group. Since they cannot go through a prolonged period of getting to know each other and of having learn-

ing occur through the interpersonal transactions in the group, outcomes must be achieved in a briefer time frame.

4. The population of the group. People with reduced or undeveloped cognitive capacity and ability to focus, such as children, people with mental retardation, and people with psychotic disorders will need structured information and activities.

As an example that ties together these various elements, I worked with a community monitoring program for youth who were involved with the juvenile justice system. As the therapist, I held a weekly group meeting for the youth. The youth moved fluidly through the community monitoring program, depending on where they were in the juvenile justice system process. Therefore, membership fluctuated each week, and it was not uncommon for members to attend only once. As a result of the open-ended format, the brief attendance of most of the participants (one to two meetings), the age of the group members (adolescent), and their problem area (juvenile offending), there was a need for a great deal of structure in the group sessions.

Under therapy groups, a particular type of group discussed by Irvin Yalom (2005), a master of group therapy, is the process group. The process group is designed for closed-ended, long-term groups in which people develop relationships over time. By processing the interpersonal patterns that emerge, people learn new ways of relating in the safety of the group. Process groups are best used with voluntary, relatively well-functioning people who are interested in the primary goal of exploring their interpersonal styles and when time to achieve a particular outcome is not limited.

Question 2.1: What treatment groups do not require as much structure?

In an outpatient agency serving dual diagnosis clients—those with both substance abuse problems and a mental illness—a group was formed for mothers who had lost custody of their children. There was no curriculum or information imparted on a formal basis; instead members discussed parenting concerns that were relevant for them that particular week. The group was described as a "support and psychoeducational group."

Question 2.2: Does the label "psychoeducational group" seem accurate? Why or why not? If it does not seem accurate, what type of group do you believe this to be?

Question 2.3: In the same agency described in the preceding question, there was a relapse prevention group for people with substance use disorders, in which the group leader presented information from a workbook that all the members had in their possession. Members would sequentially read from the workbook and then either they or other members would discuss how the information applied to them. What type of group do you think this is?

Question 2.4: In your agency, what are the types of groups that are offered? Based on the material presented in this book, do these descriptions seem accurate? Why or why not?

PURPOSE OF GROUP

The type of group must relate to its purpose, and, at the most basic level, each group must have a purpose that drives it. What do you hope people will gain from being part of your group? This concept seems basic, but occasionally student interns find themselves leading groups of which they know not the purpose. Without a determining focus, students will have no guide for interactions, and members may question and complain about why they have to attend.

Sometimes the only answer that students can come up with when thinking about the purpose of a group is that it "offers support." Support in itself is a major function of all groups, but usually such groups have other goals as well. For instance, you will be introduced to a support group for traumatic brain injury later in the workbook. Support is a primary purpose, but other purposes include educating patients and health care and social service personnel about the effects of brain injury and the resources available to help them.

One student intern discussed that at her field placement, an interdisciplinary agency that served the health and mental health needs of people with HIV and AIDS, she co-facilitated an open-ended support group that met on a weekly basis. The group discussed subjects such as loneliness and meeting prospective partners, but was based on whatever the group members brought to the group on a particular day. I asked whether it would make better use of resources if the group were run by the members themselves or with a long-term member acting as facilitator. The intern had also mentioned that although the group was generally well attended, there was a high no-show rate for clients' individual therapy sessions with their social workers. Thus, an additional alternative was proposed: the group could become treatment-oriented and deal with the type of issues currently seen in individual therapy, such as relapse prevention, "coming out" about being gay and/or having HIV/AIDS, and relationship problems. Fewer agency personnel could be devoted to individual work with clients, and resources would be used more efficiently.

Agency personnel constantly complain about high caseloads, lack of resources, and limited time to deliver services, but they need to be alert for groups, as well as other services, that are not serving a clear purpose. In addition, agencies need to use their interns well and challenge them with appropriate learning opportunities that contribute to the welfare and well-being of clients in need. Moreover, agency personnel must examine whether the purpose of the group is indeed being met (see evaluation). Finally the purpose of the group should match the problem being treated and the population being served. For example, a 10-week, closed group was held with women whose children had been placed into foster care. The goals of the group were "self-examination" and "self-acceptance."

Question 2.5: What do you think of the goals of this group, taking into consideration the problem and the time limits of the group?

Related to the purpose of the group is what you will name the group. Call the group a positive-based name that implies growth will happen rather than a deficit-based name. For instance, you would want to avoid calling a group "the depression group." A "self-esteem group" at an adolescent psychiatric unit will be discussed throughout the book. "Self-esteem" is an abstract term that is both overused and misunderstood and tends to represent a deficit focus as many people can be viewed as "lacking in self-esteem." A better focus is a topic that could be affected in a short-term group and that is strengths-based in orientation. Examples include "a coping skills group," "a feeling good group," and "a teen toolbox group." Another alternative is to have the members of the group find a name for themselves, especially when you're working with youth. This promotes members' ownership of the group.

THEORETICAL ORIENTATION

Question 2.6: What is a theory? How does theory relate to group work? Write your answer here before reading on.

Theory in the social sciences is used to explain and predict human behavior. A theory makes generalizations about observations and consists of an interrelated, coherent set of ideas and a model of how problems develop and how they can be changed. The theory of the group frames how the group will be run, what interventions will be provided, and the amount of structure to the group. See Corey (2008) for an excellent description of the different theories that can be used in group treatment, including how facilitators may use them with multicultural populations and how one may obtain further training in certain theoretical approaches.

Question 2.7: Students sometimes mention that their agencies use many theoretical orientations to group work. For instance, one person who worked with women in a prison system on substance use problems talked about a particular group being strengths-based in nature, cognitive-behavioral, and relying on an Alcoholics Anonymous model of recovery. What do you think about the approach in this specific example?

Question 2.8: Does your agency combine different theories in group work? If so, which ones? What are the advantages? What are the disadvantages? Write your answer here before reading on.

Although eclecticism (using many different practice approaches) is common in clinical practice, group leaders need to be well-versed in the theories and be able to integrate the various elements in a planful way so that material is presented clearly and coherently to the clients being served. The advantage of a theoretical framework, therefore, is that a coherent theory of change underlies the group intervention. The group purpose and how it will be achieved will generally have more clarity as a result. When there is no theory, a unifying factor underlying the various activities and discussions may be lacking, leaving clients confused about what they are learning from group. For example, the group posed in question 2.7 used both cognitive-behavioral therapy and AA-based treatment. However, these approaches may be at odds with each other: AA-based treatment follows from the disease model of alcoholism and purports that total abstinence is the goal, and the tools needed to reach the goal are group fellowship and spirituality. Work evolves through completion of the "12 steps." Cognitive-behavioral therapy helps people identify the triggers and the consequences of substance use through functional analysis of behaviors. Skills are taught to modify the triggers for use. Although these are two very different approaches, they appear to be equally effective when compared against each other (Project Match, 1997, 1998).

We will discuss, in the next chapter, how the use of empirically tested group programs promotes a clear conceptualization of the theory driving the curriculum and one that is based on available research about the population. Drawing again from question 2.7, it is well-known that prison populations of women with substance use problems typically have trauma in their backgrounds, and a focus on the trauma is necessary in order to effectively treat the substance use (Battle, Zlotnick, & Najavits, 2003). However, in this particular example, the treatment program avoided discussion of the trauma as they found that the women became "more upset and unruly" as a result.

On the other hand, many agency personnel may not see the need for theory, believing that it is too restrictive and academic. They want to be able to use different techniques and activities and not be limited by theory. An advantage of eclecticism is that people draw on practice approaches that they believe will best fit their clients; in other words, they may individualize the group intervention to fit client needs.

GROUP CURRICULUM

Question 2.9: How is the theory of the group related to its curriculum? Write your answer here before reading on.

The curriculum (also often referred to as a group treatment "manual") derives from its theoretical framework. For instance, cognitive-behavioral groups for anxiety disorders have, at their center, the importance of exposure (exposing clients to the anxiety-inducing object or event so that the anxiety eventually dissipates). As a result, such a curriculum will present information on anxiety disorders and how avoidance (leaving or avoiding anxiety-provoking situations) reinforces anxiety. Coping strategies are presented so people can better manage their anxiety, and a method to expose the client to the anxiety will be explored (Bieling, McCabe, & Antony, 2006).

Question 2.10: How have you or your agency gone about developing or finding a curriculum for a group?

Many students and professionals end up creating their own curricula, compiling activities that seem to meet the general purpose of the group, or adapting curricula already present in their agencies. This was certainly how I went about putting together curricula for group work in the past. However, many curricula have already been developed. Why spend all that time and effort, not to mention agency resources, in putting together a curriculum when experts have already devised manualized group interventions that have been tested?

Additionally, mandating bodies in the social work profession state the need for relying on interventions that have an evidence basis. The National Association of Social Workers, 1999, Code of Ethics states: "Social workers should critically examine and keep current with emerging knowledge relevant to social work and fully use evaluation and research evidence in their professional practice" (5.02 Evaluation and Research, c). Another mandating body in social work, the Council on Social Work Education states that direct practice content in schools of social work should include "…identifying, analyzing, and implementing empirically based interventions designed to achieve client goals" (Council on Social Work Education, 2004, p. 10)

Aside from these mandates, there are other advantages to relying on empirically tested interventions. Social work practitioners and the agencies in which they work may be held increasingly accountable for client outcomes, with fee reimbursement for services dependent on the use of empirically based treatments. Grant funding may also require that interventions be reliant on an evidence basis. Second, other mental health professions (e.g., medicine and psychology) have increasingly turned to empirically based treatments. In order to be both competitive and conversant with the other helping professions, social work practitioners must possess knowledge of and skill with empirically based treatment.

The highest line of evidence in determining the research support behind interventions is the *systematic review* (Petticrew & Roberts, 2006), which aims to comprehensively locate and synthesize the treatment outcome literature that bears on a particular question. If the systematic review lends itself to *combining* the results of primary studies in a quantitative way, then it is a *meta-analysis*. Meta-analysis involves statistical techniques for aggregating the quantitative results of different studies in the same area.

Meta-analysis offers a number of advantages over looking at results of individual studies. Many times individual studies present contradictory results (e.g., one study reports statistically significant positive results, another presents non-significant results), so it is difficult to know overall how well the intervention works. Studies also vary by sample size, type of research design used and other methodological features, as well as the demographic characteristics of the sample and intervention variables. Inconsistencies between studies can be addressed by putting the quantitative results of each study in a standardized form called the *effect size,* which are then combined for each study to create an overall effect. The effect size indicates the strength of the relationship between variables, for instance between a particular type of intervention and the outcome of interest. An effect size of zero thru .20 is considered negligible, .20 thru .50 small, .50 thru .70 moderate, and over .70 large (Cohen, 1988). In other words, the larger the effect size, the greater the impact of the intervention.

Given the evidence that can be provided by systematic reviews and meta-analyses, a social worker interested in knowing if group intervention is effective, and what types of group intervention are particularly helpful, can run the search terms "systematic reviews" and "meta-analysis" with the area of interest. Databases within which to run searches include the following:

- *Cochrane Collaboration, which synthesizes results of studies on effects of interventions in health care (see www.cochrane.org)*
- *The Campbell Collaboration, which synthesizes results of research on interventions in the fields*

of social care education, social welfare, mental health, and crime and justice (see www.campbellcollaboration.org)

- *The Database of Abstracts of Reviews of Effect (DARE) maintained by the Centre for Reviews and Dissemination at the University of York (UK) (see http://www.york.ac.uk/inst/crd/crddatabases.htm)*

- *Psychinfo, which is probably the most useful of the library databases for finding group interventions*

- *CINAHL (Cumulative Index to Nursing and Allied Health Literature)*

- *ERIC (Education Resources Information Center)*

- *Medline/Pubmed (biomedical literature)*

- *Social Work Research Abstracts*

- *Social Services Abstracts*

- *Sociological Abstracts*

If there are no systematic reviews or meta-analyses in a particular area, then the next best avenue is to search for a *literature review*. A literature review is a narrative summary of the literature. Generally, a literature review still holds advantages over examining individual studies, which have been done in a particular area, but they do not have the rigor of systematic reviews or meta-analyses.

In order to understand the process of searching for and interpreting reviews, let's use an example involving social skills training. Social skills training is often offered on a group basis in school settings to children with emotional or behavioral disorders. Running a search on this topic with "meta-analysis" yields the following study:

Quinn, M., Kavale, K., Mathur, S., Rutherford, R., & Forness, S. (1999). *A meta-analysis of social skill interventions for students with emotional or behavioral disorders*. Journal of Emotional and Behavioral Disorders, 7, 54-64.

Reading the article, you learn that social skills training (most of which was conducted in schools and in a group modality) showed a negligible effect (0.199) with children with emotional or behavioral disorders. The authors examined various factors related to outcome but were not able to recommend any particular type of program.

Question 2.11: What is your conclusion from seeing this research? How do these findings inform what you will do in your school system in terms of social skill training?

Let's use a different example involving the school setting—this one targeting youth anger. In a meta-analysis of 21 articles, the mean effect size on anger was .54, and the mean effect on social skills was .34 (Gansle, 2005). Interventions (and they were mostly offered in groups) that used discussion, modeling, role play, and practice were associated with better outcomes. Additionally, programs that centered on social aspects of anger, such as communication skills, social skills, and social problem-solving, performed better than interventions that were more self-focused, involving feeling identification and management, as well as relaxation, visualization, and imagery.

Question 2.12: Based on this meta-analysis, what do you conclude about the use of school-based programs targeting youth anger? What do you make of the effect size on social skills when comparing it to the previous meta-analysis we discussed above? How would you go about selecting a group intervention for middle school youth with anger problems?

Question 2.13: You could argue at this point: This is not a research class. Why are we talking about this kind of information here? Try to answer this question yourself, giving both sides of the argument: Why we should talk about it here and why we should not. Write your answer below.

Meta-analyses flag the studies that are included in the analysis, so that one can find those that have high effect sizes and/or are representative of the studies that have shown effectiveness. Once these studies have been identified, then you can look them up in academic databases and discover whether the authors have a curriculum that is available free of charge or that can be bought inexpensively. One note is that more recent studies tend to have a higher likelihood of including citations for manualized treatment.

In your school district, recently an expensive "social skills" program has been purchased for implementation with students who have been classified as "emotionally disturbed." Interest in the program was initially generated by a small group of school social workers who attended a conference in which the developer of the program presented his model of intervention. The presenter reported that the program had proven effective in research, although did not specify the research. The social workers were so impressed with the program developer's presentation that they persuaded the head of the special education department to adopt the program.

Question 2.14: Did you see anything that you, as a social worker, might have done differently in the previous situation?

Question 2.15: Select an area in which you are interested in running groups. Run relevant database searches, crossing your particular descriptives against "meta-analysis" and "systematic review." Were you able to find one? What did it tell you? Do you see anything that you, as a social worker, might have done differently in this situation?

Question 2.16: Within the systematic review or meta-analysis, find the individual studies that have a high effect size and that have been implemented in groups. From these studies, see if you can locate the curriculum that will work with your group.

There are also other ways to find curricula:

- Search for studies of group treatment in your area of interest. The curriculum that was used could be described in an article or a book you can obtain. Alternatively, the authors might mention you need to write to them to obtain the curriculum. If no information is provided about the curriculum, you can e-mail the first author (e-mail addresses of the primary author of a study are now routinely provided; you can find them through their affiliation at their institution).

- Certain government agencies, such as Substance Abuse and Mental Health Services Administration have available a compilation of evidence-based treatments, some of which are offered in a group modality.

- Conduct a Google search for group treatment (or therapy), your topic area, and curriculum. Some curricula are downloadable for free; others are commercially available. You must be aware of those you have to pay for as not all of them have been assessed through research, and they can be expensive. Appendix 1 compiles a selected list of empirically supported group curricula for different problem and population areas that are either free or low-cost.

Question 2.17: Using these other methods above, see what other curricula are available for your topic of interest.

A point worth mentioning is that curriculum implementation must follow from the problem, population, and length of treatment for which it was designed. The school system in which one social work intern was placed purchased a dropout prevention package for youth with learning disabilities and implemented it for youth with emotional disabilities in order to improve social skills. The social work intern evaluated the impact of the groups and found that, on a school system level, there was no difference in attendance and disciplinary referrals from one year when the program was not in existence and the next when it was implemented on a school system-wide basis. Perhaps the program would have had a chance to be successful if it had been administered as designed with the target population.

Question 2.18: A school system purchased a research-based, 12-session substance abuse prevention group program designed as a universal program (offered to all students in the school). The group program was used on a six-session basis with youth who had been charged with a substance-related offense on school grounds (i.e., they were already substance using). Do you believe this program achieved the desired outcome? If not, why?

SUMMARY

In this chapter, we have covered classifications of groups, their purpose, theoretical orientation and its link to curriculum. Students and social work professionals can maximize the effectiveness of groups if they give careful attention to these elements. I particularly want to stress the importance of using pre-tested curricula. If you use pre-tested curricula, you will likely have a clearer understanding about the theoretical orientation of your group and its relevance to the population and problem with which you are intervening. Not only that, valuable agency time and other resources will not be expended on creating curricula that might not be as effective with the population and problem you are working with in groups.

Chapter 3
Setting Up Groups

When students bring up problems that occur in groups, these often relate to the way the group has been set up initially. For that reason, Chapter 3 discusses the planning of groups. Some essential elements, such as types of groups, theoretical orientations, and curricula, have already been discussed in Chapter 2. This chapter will cover other important aspects of planning.

- Group leadership
- Group size
- Recruitment and screening for appropriate group composition
- Open-ended versus closed-ended groups
- Group duration
- Group setting
- Putting it all together

GROUP LEADERSHIP

Critical facets of group leadership include the stability of the leadership and the decision to have single or co-leadership. In considering co-leadership of groups, we will examine the advantages and disadvantages of such a leadership style. If you do choose co-leadership, we will talk about how to construct it so that leaders work together well and learn from each other.

Stability in Group Leadership

An obvious aspect of group leadership that one might assume but sadly does not always take place in practice, is stable group leadership. Is there a leader (or co-leaders) who can be present for every session of the group that is held? If a leader or co-leaders are assigned to start a particular group, everything must be done in his/her and the agency's power to ensure that they remain as the leaders. In an adolescent acute inpatient hospital, a student intern described how group leaders rotated daily between the various groups (and the program mainly relied on group services). Since members typically only participated in the inpatient treatment program for a week (although some stayed for several weeks), why couldn't they rely on the same person running each particular group on successive days? Trust in group leadership is an essential element of functional groups. Members will not know if it is safe to disclose and to risk vulnerability and new patterns of behavior in a group when they are not sure if they can trust the leader. This process of trust takes awhile to build.

In the following excerpt, the social work intern is left alone to run a treatment group with adolescents

ages 15-18 in a residential treatment program when the leader has left on an "emergency." Group lead-
ers were often called out of groups in this facility to meet with doctors or to manage a crisis with a client.

Intern:	Let's continue the discussion, who has something else to share?
Group member #1:	Hey, what about you? Do you have a relationship?
Group member #2:	Yeah, tell us about your relationships.
Intern:	What do you mean?
Group member #1:	Do you have a boyfriend?
Intern:	No.

(All of the following questions come fast.)

Group member #3:	Okay, then, but have you had boyfriends in the past?
Group member #2:	Yeah, how many guys have you kissed?
Group member #1:	How old were you when you lost your virginity?
Group member #3:	How many guys have you slept with?
Group member #1:	What was it like?
Group member #2:	How did you know when it was right?
Group member #4:	Tell us all about your sex life.
Intern:	This group is really not about me and my relationships, it is more for you to talk about yours and how you handle them. Let's try to keep the focus on you and not on me.
Group member #2:	How is that fair? We come in here and share information that you get to listen to, but you won't share any information with us about you. I'm just not talking anymore either. This group isn't about me.
Group member #3:	Yeah, that's right. I'm not sharing anymore either.
Group member #4:	Me either.
Group member #1:	Ditto.
Intern:	I can see how this may seem unfair to you, but these groups are for all of you and not a time for the leaders to share information about themselves. Let's go back to an interesting question you asked me that I want to ask all of you, how do you know when it is right or not to sleep with someone?

(At that point, the group members refused to talk for the remaining five minutes of the session.)

Question 3.1: How could the group have been set up initially to avoid an interaction such as the above?

Katie, a new therapist is being introduced to an established evening therapy group, which is comprised of about 15 members. The group is comprised of mentally ill adults, both men and women, between the ages of 25 and 60. The group's regular therapist, Dara, is frequently out, and Sara, the department supervisor, and Katie will be working together until Dara returns.

Sara: Okay, everyone, I want to introduce you to Katie. She's going to be working with me for a while.

Katie: Hi!

Group: Hi.

Sara: Tonight we're going to start off working together so we can all get to know each other and then later we'll split the group into two, and half of you will go with me and the other half will go with Katie. Okay?

(Group nods and snickers)

Ellen: Katie, what kind of credentials do you have?

Katie: I have a bachelor's degree in psychology, and I also work here during the day. I work in the Social Rehabilitation program, which is basically...

Ellen : *(interrupting)* I know what Social Rehab is.

Katie: Oh, okay. Good.

(Katie takes the group on her own.)

Katie: Okay, let's get started. I'd really like to hear from each of you for a few minutes tonight so that I can really get a chance to get to know all of you. Would anyone like to start? *(pause)* Ellen? Would you like to start?

Ellen: I don't have anything to say.

Katie: Well, just start by telling me something about yourself.... Anything.

Ellen: There's nothing to tell.

Katie: Nothing?

Ellen: Look, I've been in this group for six months and I haven't gotten any better. And the therapists keep changing! And I'm tired of having to tell my story over and over again!

Katie: I can understand that that would be very frustrating.

Ellen: And, no offense, but I don't see how you're going to help me if no one else can!

Katie: Sometimes it helps just to have someone to talk to. And that's actually one of the benefits of group since I'm not the only person here. You have everyone else in the group to help you too.

Ellen: Just go on to the next person.

(Later in the evening, during a break, Katie notices that Ellen is upset and crying, as she sits outside smoking a cigarette, and goes out to speak to Ellen.)

Katie: Hi, Ellen. You seem upset, what's going on?

Ellen: Nothing.

(Ellen gets up and walks away.)

Katie: Is there anything you want to talk about?

(Ellen continues to walk around the courtyard in circles; Katie, in an attempt to connect with Ellen, continues to sit in the courtyard.)

Katie: I'm just going to sit here for a while, so let me know if you want to talk.

(Ellen continues to walk in circles, without acknowledging Katie.)

Katie : *(after about 5 minutes)* Ellen, I'm going to go inside now and start up the group again. Come join us whenever you're ready, okay?

(At the end of the night Ellen asks to speak to Katie and Sara.)

Ellen: The thing is that the doctor told me when he put me in this group that he was going to make sure I got into Dara's group because he said, "She's really good." But I'm never in Dara's group. I haven't been in her group in weeks, even when she's here!

Sara: I appreciate you coming and talking to us about this. It's just kind of hard having Dara out so much. We've been trying our best to switch the groups evenly between us when she is here.

Ellen: I know, I know. And it's nothing against you, Katie.

Katie: No, it's okay.

Ellen: I just would like to be in Dara's group as much as I can, if that's possible.

Sara: Well, I don't want to give you a definite answer, but we'll try to work it out.

Ellen: Thanks. It's really nothing against you, Katie.

Katie: It's okay; see you next week, Ellen.

Question 3.2: What's positive about the way the group facilitator, Katie, handled this? What's the main problem going on in this scenario?

Question 3.3: What other ways could this have been approached?

A student intern described being part of a six-week substance abuse treatment group for adolescents who had been guilty of a substance-related transgression on school grounds (bringing a drug to the school, being under the influence in school, and so forth). She said that although the main facilitator remained the same each weekly session, the co-leader position would rotate between the different student interns (three). When questioned about this style of group leadership, the student intern denied that it had a negative impact on the group's functioning because the youth "didn't take it seriously anyway."

Question 3.4: What is your reaction to a group being led in this fashion? What is your reaction to the student intern's response?

Co-Leadership

Question 3.5: What are the advantages and disadvantages of co-leadership? Write your answer here before reading on.

There are many potential advantages to co-leadership (Yalom, 2005):

- Two people provide a greater cognitive (e.g., can generate more hunches and strategies) and observational (e.g., one person can attend to process, the other content) range.
- The leaders can play different roles (e.g., one can present the material, one can help members with the activity).
- The leaders bring different perspectives, backgrounds, and personalities, and, in this way, can complement each other.
- Leaders can use their interactions for modeling, (e.g., appropriate ways to show disagree-

ment, respectful language, acceptance of others, adherence to group rules).

- They can provide feedback to each other on leadership performance and reactions to group members.
- Poses practical advantages—in the event of illness, or if someone has to leave the room.
- Can offer support and encouragement in dealing with group leadership challenges. One of these special challenges involves handling group members' anger. A co-leader can help the other leader "to weather a group attack upon oneself and to help the group make constructive use of it" (Yalom, 2005, p. 445).
- In the special case of male-female co-leaders, "the image of the group as the primary family may be more strongly evoked; many patients may benefit from the model setting of a male-female pair working together with mutual respect and without the destructive competition, mutual derogation, exploitation, or pervasive sexuality that they too often associate with male-female pairings" (Yalom, 2005, p. 444).
- Between the two of them, co-leaders can model for the group certain skills they are teaching.
- Co-leadership is a way that beginning group leaders can gain experience under the mentorship of a more experienced person.

In their internships, students can ideally take the role of co-leader with an experienced group leader. As agency resources are typically stretched too thin to allow for experienced social workers to act as co-leaders with each other, this might be one of the few situations co-leadership takes place in current practice.

Unless students have had prior experience leading groups before their placement, I suggest they co-lead groups rather than assume sole leadership. I have seen students being placed in difficult situations because they are in the position of being the sole leader. Worse, I have seen them offer inappropriate service because of their level of experience.

Possible disadvantages of co-leadership do exist (Yalom, 2005). First, if there is a problem in the co-therapy relationship, then the group may suffer. More specifically, group leaders could work at cross-purposes to each other because of their differing personality styles, their theoretical orientation, or because of competition. Additionally, a co-leadership team can reinforce harmful stereotypes (such as the subservient female or minority leader).

If there is to be a co-leader, particularly one from a host setting in which social workers are employed (a hospital, school, criminal justice agency), there needs to be clear expectations about what the group will entail. An opening to a discussion can proceed from the following type of statement, "I have ideas about how the group could be run, but I wanted to hear from you about what you were thinking."

One student intern placed in a school setting was disappointed with a group she was co-leading with a health educator for pregnant and parenting teens. She had envisioned a group in which educational information would be shared with the group, but also thought discussion of the girls' feelings and challenges would be shared authentically. Instead, she found that the students sat in rows, her co-leader presented information in a lecture-type format, and the girls remained silent, even when the intern asked questions that would require the group members to process feelings or experiences.

She had made assumptions about how the group would be run but had not discussed these before-hand with the other leader.

A further problem with co-leaders involves the resources represented by two agency personnel co-leading the group. In addition to the group time itself, there is also the time associated with planning sessions (what will be covered during the session, what activities will be presented to the group) and coordinating roles and tasks (who will pull together the materials, who will provide educational information, who will process the activities. It is necessary to have adequate planning to coordinate roles and activities in order for the group sessions to run smoothly, to cover all the necessary information, and to avoid having two co-leaders work at cross-purposes with each other. Sufficient time to process the group together afterward allows for evaluation of the activities that took place, the progress of group members, and the performance of the leaders.

A final potential disadvantage exists when co-leadership structure replicates stereotypical patterns. For instance, a person from a minority race or female gender must not be placed in a subservient role to a person of dominant race or a male, respectively. Pains should be taken so that new roles are modeled for group members to experience (Hepworth et al., 2006).

Question 3.6: How can you ensure that when you work with a co-leader, you can give each other diplomatic feedback about your performance?

The following excerpt was from a "morning meeting" group that was held in a special education school with ten 12- to 14-year-old students in the seventh grade. Morning meeting served as a daily check-in to discuss upcoming events for the day and progress toward goals that have been behaviorally defined for each student. The group was led by a teacher (Mrs. J.) and one of the school's social workers.

Social Worker:	Okay, we're doing our check-ins. Who would like to go first? Okay, thanks for raising your hand.
John:	Good morning, my goal is "I will accept redirection." My weekend was good. I got a new pair of shoes. I didn't come to school yesterday.
Social Worker:	Yes, we missed you. What happened?
John:	I don't know...uhh...I had a sinus infection.
Mrs. J.:	I know your mom lets you stay home when you want, and I bet you went out and got those new shoes yesterday.

Social Worker: Well, John, we've talked with you and your mother about your attendance, and how you need to come to school so you can learn. You have had several absences this school year. I think it's about 18 or so. Part of the reason you don't get the lessons is because you've had so many absences.

Question 3.7: Having read this scenario, what would be your feedback to your co-leader if you were the social worker?

Let's say you are a social work intern and you had an initial agreement with your co-leader (your field supervisor) that together you would plan for group in advance and debrief after every group sessions. What if your co-leader, for scheduling reasons, became unavailable over time to do this? You found yourself taking an increasingly backseat role in the group, deferring to your supervisor. You also found that the presentation of information and activities wasn't going smoothly because your co-leader was trying to work with information you had prepared and she was not sufficiently familiar with it.

Question 3.8: How would you approach this situation? Give your rationale?

Question 3.9: What if the original arrangement in your agency was that you would act as co-leader in a group, but at the last minute, your field supervisor told you that there was no one available to co-lead the group with you and that you would have to do it alone. You have had no experience leading groups before. How would you respond in this situation? Why?

GROUP SIZE

Question 3.10: What is the ideal number for a group? Write your answer here before reading on.

The optimal size of a group depends upon its purpose, the duration, and what type of group it is. For example, an educational group can be larger than a therapy group because the provision of information is the main aim. In general, however, seven to ten members have been referenced as ideal (Yalom, 1995).

Question 3.11: List the advantages and disadvantages of either small or large groups. Write your answer here before reading on.

There are advantages and disadvantages to small and large groups (Hepworth et al., 2006). For large groups, the advantages are the following:

- More ideas, skills, and resources are generated by the group members
- There is greater potential for learning because of role models
- There is more opportunity for support, feedback, and friendship
- Fewer difficulties exist when members are absent

A social work intern co-led an eating disorder group with 15 members. The group members complained because they had difficulty getting "group time" to talk about their concerns. However, people didn't want to quit the group because they found it more helpful than their individual sessions; the group had a lot of "energy" because of the number of members, and the women said they learned a lot from hearing about other people's issues with eating and weight.

The disadvantages of large groups are the following:

- Easier for members to withdraw or hide "in the crowd"
- Less individualized attention is available for members
- More danger of harmful subgroups forming
- Less pressure to attend; absences more likely to go unnoticed
- More difficult for the facilitator to manage
- More difficulty achieving cohesiveness

For small groups, the advantages are the following:

- Group members are more comfortable expressing themselves

- More time is available for members to engage in self-disclosure
- Less likelihood of disruptive cliques developing
- Greater attendance rates as members feel more pressure to attend
- Easier for group leaders to manage

The disadvantages of small groups are:
- Less opportunity for interaction with fewer interaction members (Yalom, 2005)
- Individuals who are anxious or shy may be uncomfortable in a small, intimate group setting in which there are greater demands for participation

From a cost/benefit perspective, a small group might be too expensive for many agencies. Because agency personnel often talk about lack of resources and overloaded caseloads, small groups do not seem to be the best use of available resources.

If too small, which could happen if you start with five or fewer members and one or more drop out, or if absenteeism is a problem, you may end up with a few individuals rather than a "group" (i.e., group cohesiveness is never achieved).

Students will sometimes report leading groups in which there are two to three members. Often, these groups will also have two facilitators, such as the student intern as well as an employed social worker. These are not so much groups as individual therapy in a group setting.

One student played an observer role in a psychoeducational relapse prevention group for people with both substance abuse and mental disorders. The group was comprised of 30 people, and about 5 of the members were sleeping. Only a couple of members were actively discussing the information the group leader provided that session on triggers for substance use. Undoubtedly, medication might have played a part in the members' nodding off; however, the large size of the group was probably to blame for some members' feelings of alienation and anonymity. The fact that the group leader and/ or other group members allowed this behavior to continue "unnoticed" only served to reinforce it.

Please note that in planning a group, recruit more members than you think you might need. The reason is that often people referred to a group do not actually attend. If you plan for the exact number you want in the group, you may inevitably fall short, taking into account people who do not come to group initially and those who drop out. We will talk more in the next section on recruiting, as well as screening members, for group.

RECRUITMENT AND SCREENING FOR APPROPRIATE GROUP COMPOSITION

Question 3.12: In your agency, how are people recruited into group?

There are several different methods for recruiting clients into group and different combinations are used in practice. Many agencies primarily rely on group services, such as substance abuse treatment centers; therefore, as potential clients go through intake, they are referred to the appropriate group offered at the agency. Other agencies recruit clients from clinicians' individual client caseloads. Group members are sometimes recruited by contacting a referral base, such as teachers in a school setting about which children in their classrooms are showing behavior problems. Child protective service workers may be asked about teens from their caseload, who are appropriate, for example, for an independent living group.

One recruitment technique is to post announcements in places where potential clients might congregate or where people who might refer clients may see them. These places may include community agencies, places of worship, public housing projects, and government benefits' offices. An alternative for recruitment is to place advertisements in local newspapers or newsletters. Web sites of organizations can also be a place to broadcast upcoming groups.

Recruitment of clients is not the only challenge in forming a group; another is to screen clients to determine their appropriateness for group.
The main criterion for appropriateness is whether the client has the problem the group is designed to address. Some of the other criteria have to do with demographic characteristics, such as age, gender, socioeconomic status, and race. We will explore some of these characteristics through example exercise.

Question 3.13: In your agency, how are people screened for their appropriateness for a particular group?

The following example involves an anger management group, which consists of about 80% court-appointed members. This closed-ended group is currently on week 3 of 18 weeks. The group is comprised of three females and twelve males. There are two co-facilitators.

Facilitator One:	Okay everyone, we briefly touched on this last week, but we are going to spend a good part of the discussion tonight talking about compassion. Compassion plays a big part in the technique that we will all be learning. To get started, I would like to ask what does the word compassion mean to you?
Guy:	I guess it means being nice to someone.
Facilitator One:	Thank you, Guy. That's a very good definition. Does anyone else want to add their feelings or thoughts?
Kevin:	Actually, I think compassion is really hard to define.

Facilitator One: That's a fair and honest comment, and we are going to discuss further what compassion means.

Lisa: Well, I think compassion is easy to define. If my husband had any compassion he would know where to put his shoes when he gets home from work. It's that easy. I ask him to do it, and he says he forgets. What kind of compassion is that?

Guy: Oh my God, enough with those damn shoes already. We're sick of them.

Kevin: Yeah, who cares where he leaves his shoes? If that's your worst problem, then you're lucky. Plus, what does that have to do with compassion?

Lisa: I just want to know how to handle the situation.

Kevin: What situation? They are shoes, just shoes.

(Laughter is heard throughout the room.)

Facilitator One: I think it's important that everyone has the opportunity to say what he or she feels.

Guy: Great, all Lisa ever talks about is her husband's shoes and how mad she is about them.

Facilitator Two: Guy, you mentioned earlier how compassion was being nice to people. How can you use that in this situation?

Guy *(rolling his eyes):* I really don't know because shoes are stupid. They're not people. I have no compassion for shoes.

Lisa: It's not stupid. He won't put his shoes away. How does that show compassion?

Facilitator One: Okay Lisa, the group gave you some suggestions last meeting, but for right now, let's get back to the main discussion, and we can talk after group, okay?

Lisa: Not really, those suggestions were not very helpful. They don't work for me. I just want a simple answer. When will you will be able to help me?

Kevin: You tried them all, and they didn't work?

Lisa: Yes.

Guy: Here's one. How about not getting so mad over those shoes? I mean, come on, they are shoes.

Lisa: They are not just shoes. I need to have them a certain way. I have asked him so many times to put them in the closet, and he gives me some excuse. I have tried everything.

George: Dude, you have to chill out.

Mike: Yeah, I had a friend that was like that. She was so crazy like you, her husband left her.

Facilitator One: Thank you all for your feedback, but I think it's important that we come back to the original topic of discussion. Can everyone please turn to page 35 in their manuals? Lisa, can you come talk to me after group?

You will note that this is an anger management group and one group member, "Lisa," actually seems to have more of an anxiety problem (related to obsessing about order). This observation was confirmed by the student intern who was involved with the scenario. This instance shows the importance of people being appropriately screened, so the group does not become derailed by one member's concerns.

Question 3.14: What age range is appropriate in children's groups? Write your answer here before reading on.

For children's groups, restrict the age range to no more than two years apart (e.g., first and second graders) as development proceeds quickly in childhood; children who are separated in age may not be able to relate socially or cognitively. I worked with a co-facilitator in starting a short-term treatment group for boys who had been sexually abused. Because of the difficulties with recruiting, we included boys with a range of ages between five and eight years. However, we found that this range of ages exacerbated some of the difficulties in having boys deal with sexual abuse in terms of members acting out and failing to attend to material.

Question 3.15: Is there a minimum age to do groups with children? Write your answer here before reading on.

I have had experience leading groups with children as young as three. When I was a student intern and placed at an agency that contracted treatment services for a child welfare agency, I was a co-leader of a group for 3-year-old children who had been maltreated by their parents. The group was 45 minutes long with structured activities, including outside play time and a snack. There was also a "light" behavioral system in place (i.e., as long as the children behaved, they were allowed to pick out a prize at the end of the group from a box of inexpensive toys). This experience showed me that as long as a group is appropriately structured and there are co-leaders, children as young as three can participate.

Question 3.16: Can you include people of different genders in group? Why or why not? Write your answer here before reading on.

The appropriate gender composition of a group depends on the purpose of the group and the problem around which it centers must be taken into consideration. For instance, a group of survivors of sexual abuse might be limited to one gender. Additionally, those who have written about substance use treatment for women suggest that women-only treatment may best fit women's unique needs, such as trauma history, parenting challenges, and relationships with partners who are addicted (Ashley, Marsden, & Brady, 2003).

In general, avoid having any one type of person—of a certain gender, a certain race, a certain age, and so on (Hepworth et al., 2006), although sometimes this cannot be avoided. Just realize that you may be setting that person up as a possible "outsider." At the same time, diversity in groups (in terms of age, gender, race, sexual orientation, SES) is encouraged as people from "different walks of life" can learn from each other. People from low SES might realize that even people with money struggle with some of the same issues as themselves. Younger people may gain exposure to the elderly; the elderly may be able to pass on wisdom to those younger than themselves. By becoming intimate in groups with people from different genders, the opposite sex may be demystified, and both men and women may learn that they yearn for some of the same essential needs.

Question 3.17: Who is not appropriate for group treatment and should be screened out as a result? Write your answer here before reading on.

The answer to the question on whom to screen from group depends on the type of group. For instance, a person with schizophrenia is typically deemed inappropriate to join a group with other, more high-functioning clients. However, people with serious mental illness routinely participate in groups in other settings, such as clubhouses, day treatment programs, and inpatient hospital programs. Some of these members may even be actively hallucinating in group, but are usually allowed to attend as long as they can maintain some level of orientation to the group.

Active substance use problems are another reason people might be excluded from group treatment (aside from those devoted to substance use treatment). Many providers believe that the substance use disorder needs to be treated before tackling other problems.

Finally, people with personality disorders, particularly borderline personality disorder, might be excluded from certain groups. Because of their problems with affect disregulation and interpersonal instability, such people may be disruptive to groups. Of course, groups for people with borderline personality disorder have been designed and tested for the treatment needs of this population. (See Linehan, 1993.)

People who are suicidal may also be screened out of outpatient groups. A group is not viewed as offering sufficient support to such a person. If the group does focus on the suicidal person, it might be to the detriment of others in the group who also need help. Additionally, having a suicidal person in group may scare other group members. However, if a person is concurrently seeing an individual therapist and the suicidal ideation develops during the time he or she is in group (not at the outset), the member may be allowed to continue with group because his or her individual therapist has primary responsibility for the person's safety.

Question 3.18: Do the group facilitators at your agency do preliminary interviews with potential group clients?

Most writers on group treatment strongly recommend preliminary interviews for the following reasons (Corey et al., 1992; Hepworth et al., 2006):
- Selecting appropriate group members
- Orienting members to the purpose of the group, its curriculum, structure, style of leadership,

and the roles of the leader and group members.
- Acquainting the group leader and the potential member
- Exploring the possible risks of group participation and how to minimize risks
- Going over confidentiality and other ground rules
- Discussing fears, expectations, hopes, and ambivalent feelings

To obtain valid informed consent in writing, which includes, as well as the above information, "relevant costs, reasonable alternatives, clients' right to refuse or withdraw consent, and the time frame covered by the consent.... In instances when clients are receiving services involuntarily, social workers should provide information about the nature and extent of services and about the extent of clients' right to refuse service" (NASW, 1999, Informed Consent).

Corey (2008) states that a preliminary interview might be particularly important for clients who are from a minority culture because the assumptions of group treatment (self-disclosure and personal growth, perhaps at the expense of the family or the community) may be inappropriate for a person's cultural context. Making the assumptions explicit helps clients understand the expectations; at the same time, learning about the client's cultural context can aid the group leader in understanding how to make the group most useful for the member.

Preliminary interviews also help the non-voluntary member orient to the group. In the individual context, the group leader can connect with the member, empathize with frustration, and emphasize the choice to participate in the group (Rooney & Chovanec, 2004).

Despite the many advantages to conducting a preliminary interview, it does not often occur in practice. People who are referred to the group are usually accepted. Therefore, by de facto, those making the referral often act as a group screener. One way to make sure that the above information is covered adequately by screeners is to give them a handout outlining the following:

- The purpose of the group, its curriculum, structure, style of leadership, and the roles of the leader and group members.
- Rules for the group and guidelines for group behavior. (This topic will be addressed in its own chapter given its importance.)
- Potential risks in being in a group and how these risks will be protected.

In this way, they will be sure to present an adequate amount of information prospective to the patient upfront.

Question 3.19: A common situation is that clients do not want to attend groups. What are the reasons clients do not want to do so, and how can you address these reasons? Write your answer here before reading on.

One way of presenting some of the benefits of groups is sharing with prospective members the many possible advantages to membership (listed in Chapter 1). Some of the risks can also be shared with potential group members, and they can be invited to discuss their concerns. Be prepared to discuss how such concerns will be addressed in group. For example, if a person worries about confidentiality, you can tell the group member that you will be discussing confidentiality in group and will ask members to apply the topic to actual scenarios so that they truly understand what it entails. (See Chapter 4).

OPEN-ENDED VERSUS CLOSED-ENDED GROUPS

Open-ended groups are ones in which members are allowed to begin at any time in the group cycle; members also terminate at different times from each other, depending on when they started. Closed-ended groups are ones in which members all start the group at the same time and progress through the group together.

Question 3.20: What are some of the advantages of open-ended groups? What are the disadvantages? Write your answer here before reading on.

The advantages of open-ended groups are that new members bring fresh perspectives. Further, clients do not have to wait for services; they join a group when they are ready to do so, when motivation is high. People also may join when immediate group work/support is prescribed by a critical event or when they are in a stage of readiness for change. A further advantage of open-ended groups is that people are often at different places in the change process. Therefore, existing group members can offer insights to new members. The following example of an open-ended support group for people in early recovery from substance addiction will illustrate this dynamic.

Facilitator:	Good evening, everyone, please welcome Peter to group. Would someone tell Peter how we introduce new members to group?
Beth:	We usually ask new members questions, Peter, like why are you here?
Peter:	I had a busy weekend using, and I went through $20,000. I own a restaurant, and now I don't have money for paychecks. My wife told me if I didn't get help, she would leave me.
Eric:	What's your drug of choice? That's a lot of money.
Peter:	Coke. Yeah, I shared it around.

Eric:	That would have paid off my student loans!
Facilitator:	Any other questions for Peter?
Ann:	Do you drink, too?
Peter:	Only when I'm coming off of coke, but it's not a problem.
Buddy:	Yeah, alcohol never was a problem for me either, but now I understand that you can be cross-addicted to anything. Drinking alcohol led me back to my drug of choice, and so be aware that it could happen to you, too.
Peter:	Well, I doubt that, but I guess I am open to anything.
Beth:	Well, I have been doing drugs since high school and I have never had problems with alcohol.
Facilitator:	Any other questions for Peter?
Elizabeth:	You know, I have a lot of trouble with all this stuff...cross-addiction...the 12-steps...I mean, (to leader) you aren't in recovery, are you?
(silence)	
Elizabeth:	I mean, it's easy for everyone who works here to say what you can and cannot do, but unless you are in our situation, how can you say what is right for us?
Facilitator:	Okay, I take it that we are ready to move the discussion from Peter. Is everyone okay with that, or are there any other questions for Peter?
Eric:	No, but welcome to group, man.
Peter:	Thanks.
Elizabeth *(to leader)***:**	Could you answer my question now?
Facilitator:	I've been running group therapies for about 15 years now, and I don't discuss my personal issues. I know that frustrates some clients, but the focus needs to be on your recovery.
David:	Well, this group has been helpful to me regardless of whether you are in recovery or not. I'm grateful for these groups and that is why I'm a bit nervous about leaving today.
Ann:	I don't know if I am ready to leave later this week. I had dinner with a friend this week, and she was pressuring me to have one drink. I tried to explain the program, but she wouldn't take no for an answer. I managed to leave, but I don't think we'll be friends since I wouldn't drink with her.
Buddy:	I had trouble with some friends, too but I had an old girlfriend come back into my life and say that she is proud of me, so I'm just not going to let the guys who don't understand get me in trouble.
Eric:	I want to go back to what Elizabeth was saying about AA meetings. I got in trouble with Dorothy (program director) because I couldn't make three meetings last week because of work. I think it's easy for you guys to tell us what to do, but you aren't trying to work, too. I mean, this is your job!
Facilitator:	Well, Eric and Elizabeth seem pretty frustrated with the program rules. Is anyone having trouble following the contract that you signed at admission?
Ann:	Well, last time I was in the program I didn't follow the rules and look where it got me. So, this time I decided that I had better do what I was told.

Peter:	You were here before?
Ann:	Yes, last year. I wasn't ready then, but I think that I am now. It is difficult, though, especially when friends act the way one did this week.
Facilitator:	I hear that some of you are frustrated and fearful. I also know that most of you drank or used to bury these feelings in the past, so congratulations on making different choices here tonight and for your futures.

In this scenario, two group members challenged some of the information they received about 12-step programs and the recovery model of the treatment center; however, it was not necessary for the group leader to address their concerns; the group members who had been at the program for a longer period of time were willing to share their positive experiences with the program. For instance, David, who is preparing to leave the program, says, "Well, this group has been helpful to me regardless of whether you are in recovery or not. I'm grateful for these groups and that is why I'm a bit nervous about leaving today." Later, Ann, another presumably long-term member, said, "Well, last time I was in the program I didn't follow the rules and look where it got me. So, this time I decided that I had better do what I was told."

There are also disadvantages to open-ended groups. The instability associated with members coming and going discourages members from developing the trust and confidence to openly share and explore their problems. As a result, work is disrupted, and open-ended groups cannot proceed through the stages of group development; they typically remain at the beginning stage. However, if there is a stable core of group membership (say four to five people) that remain in an open-ended group, they are able to process through the various stages of development, which affords them an opportunity to learn about their interpersonal functioning. For example, a brain injury group held at a medical hospital had a core group of people who attended the group, although both people with brain injuries and professionals working with brain injury patients could also come to the group.

At the same time, the group leader has to be aware of some common reactions to new members coming in when there is a core group of stable participants (Yalom, 2005). The latter may fear:

- Change to status quo
- New members will slow down the group's progress.
- New members will present as rivals for the leader and the group members' attention
- New members will be a threat to their position of power in the group

Yalom's position is that these fears are unrealistic, and that new members get quickly integrated, although he generally writes about closed-ended groups. In open-ended groups, the leader can be alert to such potential reactions and might bring them to light as a part of group process.

Another potential disadvantage of open-ended groups is that each meeting needs to stand alone. That is, sessions cannot be dependent on or build upon what people might have learned in previous sessions. I have already provided the example of the open-ended group I led in the community monitoring program for juvenile offenders. Sessions had to stand alone as membership fluctuated from week to week, and it was not uncommon for members to attend only once.

A final disadvantage to open-ended groups is that consideration needs to be paid to how new group members will be oriented—otherwise, group time will be continuously taken up with orientation (introductions, purpose of group, rules, guidelines for group behavior, and so forth) and will frustrate members' progress in group. At a minimum, people can state their names at the start of group, but here are other options for conveying the rest of the information:

- Have an individual meeting with the prospective group member before the group (a preliminary interview). The advantage here is that the group member knows what to expect and can be prepared for the first group meeting. The disadvantage is that preliminary interviews are not routinely conducted in agencies.

- Have an individual meeting with the group member after he or she has completed the first group session. This method has been adapted from the Weight Watchers method of conducting orientations to their group meetings. The advantage is that staying after group is sometimes more feasible than trying to get a group leader and a potential group member to meet ahead of time. It also ensures that orientation time is spent on someone who actually comes to the group first (rather than scheduling orientations for people who never show up). Finally, it exposes people to the group so that the orientation material has some meaning to them. For instance, talking ahead of time about how the group is concerned with member-to-member interactions makes more sense after a person has seen the interaction patterns in a group.

- Posting the purpose, rules, and guidelines in a visible spot in the group room. The disadvantage is that there may be quite a bit of material to cover—too much in fact to capture on a poster sheet.

- Providing the group member with written material. The advantage is that it is cost-effective and efficient. The disadvantage is that some group members may not read the material, either because of lack of motivation or time, or because they are not literate in the language in which the material is available.

Question 3.21: What are the advantages and disadvantages of closed-ended groups? Write your answer here before reading on.

Advantages of closed-ended groups are that productive work can occur when group members are allowed to go through group stages together. Material in each group can build on each session; people can thus learn skills over time. Additionally, when people know there is a termination date, it may encourage them to work more efficiently toward goals. Some of the disadvantages of closed-ended groups are that a group may not be available when people are motivated or need services. One more potential problem is dropout may cause the group to dwindle to unacceptable numbers.

Question 3.22: How many sessions will a group hold over time? Write your answer here before reading on.

GROUP DURATION

The number of sessions comprising groups varies widely depending on the purpose and type of group. Some groups may be time limited in nature. For instance, many groups described as cognitive-behavioral are approximately 12 to 16 sessions in length (Bieling et al., 2006). Process groups may be long-term and go on for years.

The length of time that groups last over time relates to whether they are closed- or open-ended. Closed-ended groups have a specific time frame, whereas some open-ended groups allow people to attend for as few or as many sessions as needed. For instance, in support groups for family members of suicide, people may attend for only one session or they may keep coming for years. Other open-ended groups may have a curriculum of a certain length, and members remain in group until they cycle through the whole curriculum, or until the group leaders determine that they have mastered the material. For instance, an ongoing psychoeducational group was held for mothers whose children had been sexually victimized. The group comprised a 12-week curriculum on various topics, such as belief and support, sexual abuse dynamics, talking to children about abuse, assertiveness, and so forth. Women entered into the curriculum at various points, but would experience the totality of the curriculum, usually more than once, until the child welfare caseworker, in collaboration with the primary therapist, determined they were appropriately supportive of their children.

Question 3.23: Is there an ideal length of time for the group sessions themselves? Does this length differ for adults and children? How often will the group meet? Write your answer before reading on.

For adults, an hour and a half is a typical session length, but for children's shorter attention spans, 45 minutes is adequate. Some adults require shorter groups, as well. For instance, groups with people with psychotic disorders or people with mental retardation might be as short as children's groups. Generally, outpatient groups meet once a week, although inpatient and residential treatment groups might meet more often, sometimes even daily.

GROUP SETTING

The potential group leader must attend to the physical setting of the group as it "contributes to the climate of a group" (Corey et al., 1992, p. 60). The ideal group environment is a room small enough so that group members feel a sense of intimacy with each other yet do not feel crowded. Large rooms, such as school cafeterias or auditoriums, can feel impersonal. They can also be distracting, especially for children, if there is too much space surrounding the group. Additionally, for children, avoid holding group in a room full of toys and games, which will tend to be distracting. Include only those supplies that will relate to the group's activities.

Comfortable furniture—couches, comfortable chairs—are better than metal folding chairs or molded plastic. A table can create a barrier between members, so place chairs in a circle without a table in the middle. Overhead fluorescent lighting is fairly standard in many offices, but this produces an overly bright, uncomfortable light. Instead, illuminate the room with floor or table lamps with softer light to create a comfortable and less institutional atmosphere.

Privacy is an additional consideration of the setting. This may seem obvious, but the group setting cannot be a thoroughfare for non-group members. In a couple of groups I led, people extraneous to the group (caseworkers, teachers, students) walked through the middle of our sessions to retrieve items and so forth. Other personnel may not see the necessity of holding the group in a place that is held private, but it is up to you, as the social worker, to ensure that it happens.

Finally, confidentiality of other program participants is essential. My juvenile offender group was held in a room in which the names of all the other program participants were written on a dry erase board under each caseworker's names, so that caseloads could be tracked. In order to maintain confidentiality, I would erase all the names before each group (much to the caseworkers' annoyance as they would have to rewrite the names after group was over).

PUTTING IT ALL TOGETHER

Because a lot of elements go into planning, it is important to see how these all fit together. To give you some practice in doing this, an exercise is presented below.

In this group, typically three boys attend, but in this particular session only two boys are present. Youth were referred because their school Individualized Education Plan required that they have a social skills group. The duration of the group was for the entire school year. The weekly group was held in the self-contained classroom for emotionally-disturbed youth at the middle school the boys attend.

Question 3.24: In the following depiction of an open-ended social skills group, middle-school boys overhaul the planning of the group; take into account some of the limitations you see here (page 45).

Peter (to the air in general): Oh, dude, do I have to stay for this?

SW: Yes, Peter.

Intern: Hi, Jordan, hi Peter. Where's Marty today?

Jordan: Hi, SW, hi intern.

Peter: I hate these guys. Can't I leave?

SW: No, Peter.

Peter: I need to go to the office or something. Yeah, to the office.

SW: Peter, social skills group is on your IEP. You need to stay. We're going to play a board game today. Peter, do you want to participate?

(The social worker, intern, Jordan, and Peter sit at a table around a board game.)

SW: Okay, we each draw a card, and the card will have a situation on it. You read the card out loud, then tell us if the choice they made is a good decision or a bad decision. Then you turn it over, and read to everyone the answer, and how many spaces that you go for that answer. Peter, you can go first.

Peter: *(draws game card and deliberately reads it wrong to exaggerate how many spaces he should go)* Go forward 22 spaces. *(starts to move piece)*

Intern: Let's try that again, Peter. Read that again?

Peter: Oh, fine! *(moves piece back, deliberately knocking over everyone else's pieces)*

Jordan: Peter, knock it off! That's so rude! (puts pieces back)

(Peter draws another card, reads it silently and moves his piece a reasonable number of spaces.)

SW: What's the card say, Peter?

Peter: Nothing! Geez!

SW: Peter, part of the game is that we read the cards out loud so we can all learn from it.

Peter: Geez, I got it right!

SW: Yes, well next time, please read it to all of us. Jordan, it's your turn.

Peter: Hey, can I go to the drinking fountain?

(He gets up from the table. No one says anything as they are paying attention to Jordan reading.)

Jordan (reading from his card): Is this a good idea or a bad idea?

Peter: Hey, can I go get a drink?

(He leaves the room as everyone continues to pay attention to Jordan.)

Jordan: I think it's a good idea, because everyone should help with the group project. It will be a better project if everyone contributes. (turning the card around) It says "good idea, move forward 16 spaces."

SW: Good job, Jordan. Nice point. Where is Peter?

Intern: He said he wanted to go to the drinking fountain. I think since nobody said no, he took that as consent. I'll go see what's taking him so long.

SUMMARY

This chapter has given consideration to the planning of groups in order to avoid problems from cropping up during their implementation. Attention to these aspects can ensure that the group will run more smoothly and will be optimally therapeutic for its members. This chapter mentioned the topic of orienting members to how groups are run and what will be expected of them. Chapter 4 will be devoted to this topic, given its importance.

Chapter 4
Rules and Guidelines

This chapter will cover rules and guidelines for group behavior. A separate chapter is devoted to this topic, even though it is generally part of the beginning of groups (or the preliminary interview), given the importance of being clear about behavioral expectations for members and so that therapeutic norms develop in the group. Additionally, rules and guidelines are often different from the behaviors that people usually commit in various social situations, especially since people seeking group services often have interpersonal problems. Finally, certain rules, including confidentiality, the expectations for attendance and participation, and respect for others, lay an ethical foundation for the rights of people who attend groups.

Question 4.1: What rules do you think are important for the functioning of a therapy group? Write your answer here before reading on.

RULES

A way to introduce rules is to talk about the anxiety that most people feel when they are starting a new group. The rules are in place in order to create a safe environment so that people can share personal information and try out new behavior. Rules are also in place for ethical reasons—to protect the rights of group members and to inform them of their responsibilities. Note that ethical issues involving group work are not specifically delineated in the NASW Code of Ethics; ethical principles and values are laid out for social work practice in general. For a more detailed discussion of ethics that operate in group work, consult The Association for Specialists in Group Work (1998). This organization is under the auspices of the American Counseling Association, but any graduate-trained professional or student can join if interested in group intervention.

When formulating rules in a group, facilitators can avoid handing down rules in an authoritative way by soliciting member input. Even young children are capable of contributing to such a discussion as they are used to rules of conduct in formal settings, such as school. This invitation for group input begins to set the norm that group members will be responsible for their group.

As rules are agreed upon by the group, the leader can write them on a flip chart, and they can be kept as a record. Group facilitators can more fully involve children by encouraging them to color in and decorate the sheet listing the rules. The leader can prompt the members about rules that might be key for the protection of its members (e.g., "What about socializing with other group members? Do you think that would be okay?"). For future sessions, the group rules can be posted in a visible position in the room as a reminder to members of the rules operating in the group.

In some settings (such as prisons) and in some types of groups (adult anger management pyschoeducational groups), the rules will be less negotiable. Still, even in these types of groups, the non-negotiable rules can be presented in a respectful, non-dictatorial way, and there may be some choice about certain aspects of the group. An example involves a court-ordered anger management group in which two group members went to the bathroom (the rule in the group was that people were free to leave and go to the bathroom as needed) and were gone for a good portion of one group session. Eventually, one of the group leaders left the group and retrieved the two men where they had been socializing in the hallway. When they returned, the other members mentioned that the men's leave-taking had been disruptive; as a result, they came up with a new rule themselves—that only one person could go to the bathroom at a time. They had also agreed in a prior meeting that people would be allowed to bring beverages to group as long as they were responsible for cleaning up after themselves. These examples show that certain aspects of the group can be decided upon by the members, even in court-mandated situations.

Rules for successful group functioning comprise the following:

1. Confidentiality
2. Attendance
3. Participation
4. Respect for others
5. Contact with people outside group
6. Contact with group facilitator(s)
7. Touching
8. Refreshments

Also discussed will be how you, as the group leader, can handle any transgressions of rules.

Confidentiality

Confidentiality is obviously a priority for the safety of members and the functioning of the group. Members, when asked what confidentiality means, can easily state, "What goes on in group stays in group." In my experience, this concept remains at an abstract level unless the group leader poses certain scenarios that test the meaning of the term. For instance, group members can be asked,

"What if you're with your partner or with a friend, and you meet a group member in a social situation? How will you introduce the person and explain how you know him or her?" "What if you find out through being in group that you share an outside connection with another member? How will you ensure that confidentiality is maintained in this other setting?" For instance, in an eating disorder group, two of the young women discovered they were dating city police officers; one of the women had previously disclosed illegal drug activity that she and her police officer boyfriend had shared not knowing at the time that the other women also had a police officer boyfriend. Obviously, if this information got out to the police department, the group member's boyfriend could be fired. This type of situation can be posed to group members for their discussion, so they can understand some of the dilemmas that might be presented by confidentiality.

In a school setting, students can also be given various scenarios that touch upon the fact that knowing certain information about others might put them in a potentially powerful position vis-à-vis gossip. In discussing these scenarios, the importance of confidentiality cannot be overemphasized.

The limits of confidentiality are also discussed. Commonly, if people are in danger of hurting themselves or others, or child or elder abuse has occurred, group facilitators are responsible for breaking confidentiality in order to ensure members' and/or others' safety.

Finally, the leader can explore the consequences of breaching confidentiality. Typically, such breaches are discussed before the whole group. Violations might extend to the person being asked to leave the group.

Attendance

Regular attendance is encouraged as members will get more out of the group experience if they attend and participate. The group can be considered a system, which is more than the sum of its parts. Therefore, the interdependency between group members means that one person's absence can affect the functioning of the system as a whole.

Desired attendance is when people arrive on time and stay for the entirety of the group. A student intern placed at the adolescent unit of an acute psychiatric hospital described a group she observed in which some teens came late and others left early.

Question 4.2: In this situation, what are the problems with the fluid attendance pattern the intern witnessed?

People can be warned that they sometimes might feel uncomfortable in group; they might feel anxious, bored, alienated, or frustrated. However, rather than leaving or skipping sessions (or even dropping out), they may talk about their uncomfortable feelings in group. By processing these feelings, they are practicing authentic communication and maximizing the benefits of what group can offer. For instance, a group member may talk about feeling frustrated because the group members keep talking about the same topic week after week with no resolution. The group leader can reinforce this person's self-disclosure and ask others if they share the same concerns. Group members might be asked, "What needs to happen in here so that we are able to resolve some of what we came here for?" and the group can potentially move forward and bring benefits to its members.

Sometimes consequences are outlined for missing sessions. In a dialectical behavior therapy group for people with borderline personality disorder, if a person missed two sessions, he/she was no longer able to attend. Mandated groups, in particular, often have strict policies against members being tardy or leaving early, and these behaviors may be counted as absences. Often in such groups, people who arrive late are not allowed into the group after a certain time. Expect that if you have such policies, you may be tested at times. For instance, one evening a man who was attending an anger management got stuck in traffic on the way to the outpatient clinic where the group was held. As a result, he arrived ten minutes late for group (five minutes was the cut-off period). The group member explained about the traffic, insisting that his lateness was not his fault. However, the facilitator remained firm and forbade him from entering. As a result, the group member slammed the door, yelled about the injustice as he left the building, kicked his workbook all the way out to the car (in sight of the other members through the window), and sped off in his car.

Question 4.3: One of my students mentioned, after being told this story that it did not seem fair to penalize a group member because of traffic when it was so bad in the area where she lived. What is your response to her reaction?

Participation

Although participation is related to attendance, it deserves discussion of its own. The ideal for participation is that it is shared among group members. To get you started thinking about the importance of participation, consider the following scenario, which involves an open-ended sex-offender group. As part of the group treatment, members have to complete their sexual history, which is the first of 10 steps they have to present to the group. In the first step, clients talk about the extent of their involvement in various sexual activities, which include a list of 32 items and their substance use history. They also detail their offenses. When the group members and facilitations express satisfaction with the presentation, clients take a polygraph exam to verify they have told the complete truth about their sexual history. Group facilitators report back to the members' probation officers about their progress in group.

Question 4.4: In the scenario below, describe what the group members might have been told about participation upfront. Assuming there has been orientation about participation, how could it be referenced by the social worker?

Social worker:	Santos will finish his presentation today. What was he supposed to do and have ready for group?
Group member 1:	He was supposed to remember if there were any more incidences of infidelity and share them with the group.
Social worker:	Santos, I want you to be honest with the group, when was the last time you cheated on your wife?
Santos:	I was trying to remember, but I am not sure.
Social worker:	Was it this past weekend?
Santos:	No.
Group member 1:	Was it last night?
Santos *(laughing)*:	No.
Social worker:	You need to take these treatment steps seriously. If you are not honest with the group, you will fail the polygraph.
Santos:	The last time I think I was unfaithful was three months ago.
Social worker:	So you are referring to the incident with the girl who was delivering bread?
Santos:	Yes.
Social worker:	Are you sure?
Santos:	Yes.
Social worker:	Okay, since that was the final question in the sexual history step, we are ready to score Santos's presentation. What do you think?
Group member 2:	Santos, I give you an 8.5.

Social worker:	Why?
Group member 2:	He struggled with the step. It was hard, but I think he did a good job.
Social worker:	Okay, what do the rest of you think?
Group member 1:	I'll give you an 8 because you had a lot of difficulty answering the questions.
Social worker:	So if you think Santos struggled with the step, why are you giving him high grades? [Intern], what do you think?
Intern:	This is by far the worse presentation I have heard in the group. You have been presenting the same step for two months. You did not bother to prepare for your presentation and that is why it was so unorganized. You were not able to stay focused and answer the questions being asked. You provided too many unnecessary details.
Social worker:	Can you give an example?
Intern:	Yes, Santos, when you were asked about the last time you were unfaithful, you should have said it was about three months ago when I asked a stranger on the street if I could have her number, not go on to explain that you were driving and went to the bar that you like and could not find a parking spot so you were double parked, waiting for someone to move and then a huge delivery truck drove up, and you noticed a girl and a guy and you thought the guy was her father. But no, maybe her boyfriend and they were delivering bread. Who cares about all that unless you are trying to bore us to death? Furthermore, you do not accept responsibility for your actions; you use minimization and excuses to justify your actions. You minimize all the times you cheated on your wife by arguing that it's not that bad because she does not know, and I don't really love her, so it's okay, and who knows if she is faithful so I can be unfaithful. I don't need to get an HIV test because I feel fine, and if I feel fine I am not putting my wife at risk. Lastly, I don't know if it's your level of maturity, but you present as if everything is a joke with a smile on your face. We are talking about very serious issues and I don't think you realize that. You were dishonest throughout your presentation and had to be prompted to answer the questions and redirected continuously. I give you a 3.
Social worker:	Santos, because you received a score under seven, that means you did not pass the step and will have to do your presentation over again.
Santos:	This is bullshit! I told you what I remembered.

(Santos then lapsed into a sulking quiet)

Participation in groups might involve homework completion. Not all groups offer or require homework, but some rely heavily on its use. In a dialectical behavior therapy group, group members were required to complete homework; indeed, the beginning portion of each group was devoted to each member sharing his/her experience with the assignment. Group members were encouraged to give feedback to others during this process. When group members did not volunteer comments, the group leaders would ask open-ended questions in order to encourage participation. The group facilitators' aim was to get the other group members to reinforce and support each other when they shared homework.

Of note is that some group members may react negatively to the use of the term "homework." For example, Kohn et al. (2002), when discussing the adaptations that were made in a culturally-sensitive, cognitive-behavioral group for African-American women with depression, note that group members chose the term "therapeutic exercises" instead. There is no reason not to change the language if participants find another term more useful for them.

Respect for Others

The general rubric of "respecting others" contains many different types of behaviors. At the very least, it involves making sure that group members turn off their cellular telephones and any other electronic devices during group. "Respect" is conveyed when one person talks at a time, members listen attentively, and avoid side conversations. In the following example of an anger management group, you will see how the two facilitators responded to a side conversation.

Facilitator 1:	Okay everyone, we briefly touched on this last week, but we are going to spend a good part of the discussion tonight talking about compassion. Compassion plays a big part in the technique that we will all be learning. To get started, I would like to ask you all what the word compassion means to you when you hear it?
Guy:	I guess it means being nice to someone.
Facilitator 1:	Thank you, Guy. That's a very good definition. Does anyone else want to add their feelings or thoughts?
Facilitator 2:	George and Kevin, you two look like you are discussing something over there. Would you like to share your thoughts with the rest of the group?
George:	Not right now.
Facilitator 2:	Okay, well then, as we discussed at the beginning of the group, I know that the other group members would appreciate it if you could listen when they are speaking, and we look forward to hearing your thoughts when you are ready to share.
Kevin:	Actually, I think compassion is really hard to define.

- *Note how in this example, the facilitator referred back to the rules that were discussed at the beginning of group. Initial discussion of rules is important so that expectations are clear, and they can then be referenced.*

Contact with People Outside Group

Question 4.5: Can group members contact each other outside of group? Write your answer here before reading on.

Whether group members can contact others depends on the purpose of the group and the population with whom you're working. In some settings, people live together in residential treatment or inpatient hospitals, or go to the same school; as a matter of course, they will have contact with each other outside of group. Most groups that social workers lead have a central focus on support and will encourage friendships among members, so people can more successfully manage the problems with which they struggle. For example, mothers in a parent training group might find it helpful to have contact between sessions; in this way, they can support each other in their parenting challenges and remind each other of the skills they are learning.

Contact with Group Facilitator(s)

As with contact with other members, groups vary on the amount of contact that is allowed with the facilitator outside of group sessions. However, it is not uncommon for people to attend groups in which their individual therapist is the group facilitator, particularly in an agency setting that offers group services to its clients. Even when facilitators take pains not to play "favorites," be aware that group members may have this perception. Part of the reason is that groups recreate family dynamics; group members may relate to each other as siblings with the group facilitator as "parent." However, feelings invoked in members can be "grist for the mill"; that is, rivalry and competition between group members, when it comes up, can be processed safely in group under the leader's direction, so that people can learn about their interpersonal patterns and work to change them.

Other than the above mentioned professional contact between group members and group leaders, contact between the leader and members, for the most, is limited to within the group.

Touching

Question 4.6: Is it okay for some types of touching to be allowed in groups? What about between the group members and the group leader? Write your answer here before reading on.

In certain groups, such as those comprising members of a fragile population (people with mental illness) or those with boundary problems (people with borderline personality disorder), any kind of touching, including hugs and pats, might be seen as inappropriate and potentially hazardous to group members.

However, in other groups, members are encouraged to offer each other support, which might include hugs and pats. Sexual activity between participants is typically forbidden in groups, however, as these types of relationships will inevitably complicate the dynamics of the group (Yalom, 2005). Typically group leaders refrain from any kind of touching with clients.

Refreshments

Many times, refreshments are offered as an incentive for group attendance and are arranged by the facilitator. Other groups have rules about no food or beverages in group because of logistical concerns (such as who will clean up afterward, the fairness of one person having food if it is not offered to all) or therapeutic concerns (food or drinks could be seen as a way to deal with affect rather than dealing with it more directly in group).

Question 4.7: How will you as a group leader approach violations of group rules? Write your answer here before reading on.

Handling Transgressions in Rules

Now that you have set up all these rules, what happens if they are violated? Obviously, some transgressions are more severe than others (e.g., sexual intimacy between group members, violations of confidentiality), and some breaches of group rules are more likely to occur within the group setting, such as disruptive behaviors (e.g., talking when others have the floor). Some beginning group leaders respond that they would like to respond to any group transgressions that arise with the offending member outside of the group context. However, a guiding principle in leading groups is to handle issues within the group itself as they are shared by group members. Be explicit about this norm, so that people can take responsibility for the group's functioning. Expect that group members may approach the group facilitator individually with feedback about the way the group is run or to complain about a member. However, the standard response to these individual statements is to encourage the person to bring their concerns to the group.

GUIDELINES

After rules have been discussed, it is important to cover what I refer to as guidelines for group behavior. The time involved to explain these guidelines may be a particular concern for open-ended groups when new members may join each session. If a preliminary individual interview is not possible in these situations, then this information can perhaps be provided in handout form.

Hepworth et al. (2006) make a useful categorization of group member behaviors that fall into either help-seeking or help-giving. *Help-seeking* involves the following:

- Sharing feelings
- Asking for specific feedback (e.g., "In sharing this story, I want to know if I overreacted or if my reaction was in line with the event.")
- Being open to hearing feedback
- Being willing to try out new ways to approach problems
- Talking about the self rather than others

Notice in speech how often people use "you" as in "You were driving to the store and then this guy pulled out, and you screeched to a stop." When people do this in group, you can call their attention to it and ask them to talk from an "I" position instead as in, "I was driving to the store and then this guy pulled out, and I screeched to a stop." As well as personalizing speech, talking about the self refers to sharing personal reactions rather than talking about or criticizing others, particularly when it involves other group members. The format for doing so is essentially an "I" statement (see also communication skills): I feel [mad, sad, scared, glad] because [other person's specific behavior].

Help-giving comprises the following:

- Summarizing group members' concerns and feelings
- Asking people to be specific when they talk in generalities (e.g., "When you mention that 'people always want something from you,' to whom are you referring? Can you give a specific example?")
- Refraining from asking questions that distract the speaker and cut off further exploration (e.g., irrelevant, prying, leading, or closed-ended questions)
- Keeping people on track when they drift into tangential speech
- Pointing out strengths and giving positive feedback
- Sensitively giving negative feedback
- Refraining from premature advice giving

As a point of reference, we will delve further into the last two guidelines.

As far as giving feedback, the leader must insure that members provide it in a sensitive and authentic way to allow maximum benefit for all parties (Corey & Corey, 2006). By hearing feedback, members can gain insight about their impact on others, as well as understand more about their own interpersonal style. By giving feedback (or refraining from giving feedback), group members may also learn about the ways they relate to others in their lives. Some guidelines about giving feedback include the following:

- Show sensitivity and be as nonjudgmental as possible

- Talk in specifics about a person's behavior rather than make characterological references, by personalizing the reaction with "I" statements ("When you talk about other women like that, I feel uncomfortable and want to make sure I sit far away from you" rather than "You're a sleaze.")

The following example involves an open-ended group held in the acute psychiatric and addictions treatment unit of a hospital. The particular topic of the day was healthy family functioning. The average stay for patients in this unit is six days, although one group member, Harold, has resided in the unit for four weeks because of his participation in a medication research study.

Marcus:	Well, I never want to have anything to do with my mother. She abused me terribly, and I hate her. I want no relationship with her.
Harold:	You can't hate your mother. I don't have a mother and let me tell you, I wish I did. One day your mother might need you, and you'll need her, so don't ever say you'll hate your mother. My stepmother was abusive to me but you know what? My wife told me, "You need to stick with that woman, she might need you one day," and you know what, she did need me, and I was there for her and—
Social Worker:	Well, another way of looking at it is—
Harold:	I was saying that you never know when she might need you, and in my situation, my stepmother needed me. And, you know, I told her how I felt, but I still helped her. And you need to help people who need it, and I'll tell you, when my stepmother needed me I was there. And you can't hold no grudges in life because that person is gonna need you, and you need to be there. One day your mother might need you, and you'll need her, so don't ever say you'll hate your mother.
Social Worker:	Well, what I was going to say is that it's Marcus' choice. He's an adult.
Harold:	You have to let me finish.
Social Worker:	We've heard what you have to say, have you heard what we're saying?
Harold:	No because I'm not listening.
Social Worker:	No, you're not listening. What we're saying is that it's Marcus' choice. He's an adult. We're not condoning hatred because that can be damaging, but we don't know that his mother will need him down the line, and we need to respect his decision not to maintain that relationship.
Harold:	You keep interrupting me, and this isn't the first time. Every time I try to talk, you're trying to talk over me, and I'm not the only one who feels this way. You need to let people talk. Isn't that the purpose of the group?
Social Worker:	You need to let people talk, as well. This group is about everyone sharing their opinions and not just us listening to you talk. We heard your point, now listen to other opinions.

> **Marcus:** You know, Harold, I hear what you're saying, but my mother used to snag me with fishing hooks, and if we didn't agree with every word she said, she would punch us in the face. Once, I quoted a newspaper columnist who said that Muhammad Ali was a "paper champion," and my mother picked up a vase and threw it at me. She is the cause of many of my problems today and probably why I don't trust anybody and why I feel so nervous all the time. And so, I want nothing to do with her.
>
> **Social Worker:** And that's your choice, Marcus. It's understandable that you may not want to maintain a relationship with her. I'm not sure I would either given your descriptions of her abuse.
>
> **Marcus:** Yeah, she was terrible. I hope she burns in hell.

(At that point, Harold gets up and walks out of group.)

In this example, Harold is obviously upset when Marcus talks about "hating" his mother. After Harold's first passage of speech, the social worker could have stopped Harold and said, "Harold, what are you feeling right now?" If Harold continued on his tirade, the social worker could gently interrupt and remind him of the group guideline to refrain from criticism and instead speak about personal reactions. He could then try again, "So Harold, using an "I" statement, when you heard what Marcus was saying, how did you feel--mad, sad, scared, or glad?" Harold might then acknowledge that he was mad at Marcus for talking about his mother that way when he (Harold) did not even have a mother. The social worker might push further for some other reactions: "And how do you feel about not having a mother?" The social worker could then help Harold explore some of his feelings of sadness about this loss.

Question 4.8: What is the problem with either the group facilitator or the group members getting into advice-giving too quickly? Write your answer here before reading on.

The following provides a rationale for the importance of refraining from premature advice-giving. First, many times people already know what they are "supposed to do"; it is precisely because they are unable to follow through with this prescription that keeps them from moving forward and the reason they seek help from a group. Second, advice-giving fails to take into account a person's unique experience and situation. Telling people what they "should do" implies that we know what's best for them, when they are the experts on themselves. Third, it narrowly defines someone's options. There are typically many ways to approach a problem, and for a group member or a group leader to say, "This is what you should do," curtails the number of options available for problem-solving. Fourth, although people who are seeking help often ask, "What should I do?" telling them what to do is not the answer. They need to develop their own problem-solving skills, so they can answer this question for themselves. Fifth, offering advice can be a way of not entering into a person's experience.

For instance, in a woman's closed-ended process group, one of the members, Nicole, was describing deep feelings of depression, and group members started reeling off suggestions ("Why don't you start taking dance classes?" "I think you should quit your school program. It's not helping you feel any better." "What about moving into a nicer apartment?" and so forth). As the suggestions continued, Nicole sank lower into her chair, crying. Finally, she got up and announced she was going to the bathroom. While she was gone, the group leader asked the other group members what they were feeling. They expressed their fear that Nicole was so depressed she might commit suicide. They had been dealing with their panic about her situation by providing advice in a desperate attempt to make her feel better. What Nicole really needed, however, was to hear how scared the group members were feeling at the intensity of her pain. After she returned and the group members were able to do this, she felt validated for her experience.

Finally, Yalom (2005) states that trying to problem-solve about a person's circumstance external to the group is a difficult endeavor; the amount of information necessary for group members to understand the person's situation may use up too much valuable group time. This is a focus on the "then and there" rather than the "here and now" of the group's interpersonal reactions, which is what group has to offer that is so valuable compared to individual work.

Question 4.9: This exercise will help you consider a number of the guidelines for group behavior. Recall the excerpt from the anger management group. What guidelines have we discussed of which this group needs reminding?

SUMMARY

A focus in this chapter has been on rules and guidelines for behavior of group members. As these behaviors are often unfamiliar, the group may benefit from having attention paid to the development of these skills, which will be the focus of forthcoming chapters. For instance, talking about feelings might be advanced by having a session on how to identify feelings and how to express them in "I" messages (see Chapter 12). The process of problem-solving can be taught so that group members are better able to cope with life's challenges and so they can channel their advice-giving tendencies more productively (see Chapter 12). Specific group exercises can enhance people's ability to find strengths in themselves and others (see Chapter 11). In the meantime, however, we will turn to critical leadership skills that will help members enact these new interpersonal patterns.

Chapter 5
Basic Leadership Skills

This chapter will discuss styles of leadership and the basic skills of a group leader. The next chapter will concentrate on competencies that are typically more challenging for beginning leaders. Additionally, Chapters 13 and 14 will discuss ways to manage potentially difficult situations that may arise in groups.

STYLE OF LEADERSHIP

The particular style of leadership may depend on the format of the group. Highly structured interventions, such as psychoeducational approaches, rely on the guidance and direction of the leader, but less structured approaches encourage members to take full responsibility for the purpose, goals, and interventions used in the group (Toseland & Rivas, 2009). In many groups, the facilitator essentially does individual therapy with one group member at a time. An example of this style of leadership is exemplified in the inpatient group treatment offered at the acute hospital setting (see pages 57-58). In this style, there is intensive leader-to-member interaction with other members saying little during the exchange. This type of leadership style, though not uncommon in practice, is ill advised; it fails to take advantage of the potential benefits of the group wherein the members take responsibility for the interactions. In the example of the inpatient therapy group with Harold and Marcus, Harold might have received valuable feedback from the other group members and/or he would have heard about other members' struggles with relationships with parents who had been maltreating.

Although one person might take center stage of any group for a portion of time, the leader can generalize the work to the group. For example in the woman's process group, the group leader says after a period of concentrated work with one of the members, Nicole, "We have been talking about the need for Nicole to get more support from other women when she is feeling lonely and reaches out to men for companionship. She then ends up feeling hurt after they have sex that doesn't fulfill her emotional needs. Are there others in here who can relate to what we've talked about today? Nicole has agreed to call at least two other members of this group when she feels lonely. Does anyone else want to agree to do this, as well?"

Overall, the leader's responsibility is to see that each person gets roughly equal attention in the group rather than one group member dominating with his or her problems each week. However, some leaders would say that it is the group members' responsibility to insure they get the time they need. For example, in the 15-member eating disorders group, when people complained about the size of the group and insufficient time to talk about their concerns, the group leaders said it was up to them to assertively get their needs met.

Question 5.1: What is your reaction to this response from the eating disorders group leaders?

FACILITATIVE SKILLS

There are some basic facilitative skills that group leaders must demonstrate so that members will share their experiences and feel understood. First, the group leader needs to respond empathically to members' concerns. The leader helps members overcome feelings of alienation, stigmatization, and isolation by validating, affirming, and normalizing their experiences (Toseland & Rivas, 2009). The group leader also facilitates members' hope in the future and motivates members to make changes through the mutual aid available in groups.

We will now take a closer look at the following leadership skills:

1. Attending skills
2. Asking questions
3. Allowing the group to have ownership
4. Finding commonalities and making linking statements
5. Structuring group material
6. Providing Information in a collaborative way
7. Structuring activities
8. Reinforcing desirable group behaviors

ATTENDING SKILLS

The ability to convey effective listening through body language and verbal communication is an essential skill in all types of helping relationships, as well as for group facilitation. The practitioner must listen empathically to clients' concerns, reflecting the content of the client's messages, as well as their feelings. In this way, the individual feels heard and understood, thoughts and feelings are clarified, and other group members learn about how to listen and respond to other people's concerns.

Since we are focusing on skills of particular salience to group work, we will touch on one particular technique, the use of "scanning" (as cited in Toseland & Rivas, 2009). When a facilitator scans the group, he or she makes eye contact with all the members, rather than directing attention at one or two people. This makes people feel as if the leader is interested in them and is including them in communications. It is easy for a group leader to stay locked in eye contact with someone he or she knows well (such as a client seen in individual therapy) or someone who seems particularly interested in the material, but the group leader must include everyone in his or her gaze, even those who seem disengaged or hostile.

In this scenario involving an open-ended sex offender group, devise reflective responses after each time the featured group member speaks, (you may write your answers in the space provided following the scenario). Recognize, that this exercise is for practice; you may not want to reflect that often as it may sound unnatural or forced. For now, do not attend to the questioning of the group leader. This will be the focus of an upcoming exercise.

The group leader begins by asking the group member to describe his family and how he gets along with them.

Group member 1:	I don't get along with anyone in my family. They all hate me.
Group member 2:	What about your brother? Didn't you say that you and he get along?
Group member 1:	Yeah, he was the only one who loved me, but he died when I was eight.
Group leader:	Who hates you?
Group member 1:	My mom and the rest of my family.
Group leader:	What has your mom done that makes you believe that she hates you?
Group member 1:	When I was little, she locked me in a closet, or sent me away. She called me bad names.
Group leader:	Why did your mom lock you in the closet?
Group member 1:	She made me stay in the closet when she had men over. Sometimes I would cry and yell and she'd get really angry—she told me I had to be quiet because that's how she earned money to buy food and clothes.
Group member 3:	Did you know what was going on?
Group member 1:	Yes, I could see everything from the keyhole in the closet door.
Group leader:	Where were your brothers and sisters when you were locked in the closet?
Group member 1:	They were at my grandma's house.
Group leader:	So you were all alone in the closet?
Group member 1:	Yeah, because my brothers and sisters lived with my grandma. I was the only one who lived with my mom.
Group member 4:	How come you didn't live with your grandma?
Group member 1:	Because they all hated me—I was different.
Group leader:	How did you feel that you were different?
Group member 1:	I had a different dad.
Group member 4:	Because your mom was a whore?
Group member 1:	NO! Because my mom was raped.

Group leader:	Okay guys, Carlos is sharing some really personal and painful things with us—it's important to show him the same respect that you expect when you're sharing. Carlos, it takes a lot of courage to be open about these difficult things that have happened with you. It sounds like being locked in the closet, and seeing your mom with men, and being treated like an outsider by your family were all really hard things that you had to deal with. Can you talk about what things were like for you when you didn't have to be in the closet? How did your mom treat you?
Group member 1:	Well, she never hugged me or kissed me or acted like she loved me. But she was really nice to my brothers and sisters.
Group member 3:	Why do you think your mom treated you differently?
Group member 1:	I don't know—sometimes she said I looked like my dad.

Question 5.2: Devise reflective responses for each time a group member speaks.

ASKING QUESTIONS

Asking questions is another basic helping skill. As you probably already know, helpers strive to ask open-ended questions; that is, not answerable with a yes or no response or a one-word answer, but one in which the individual can respond in a variety of ways and explore further. In general, we avoid the following types of questions:

1. Closed-ended (those that can be answered with a one-word or brief information response. Example: "How many sisters do you have?" when a group member talks about a difficult relationship with a particular sister.

2. Leading (those that pressure the speaker to respond in a certain way). Example: "Did you enjoy the attention?"

In the following group scenario with adolescent sex offenders, identify the leading questions, the closed-ended questions, and the open-ended questions.

Group leader:	So, what do you mean to stay away from little kids? All little kids in every situation?
Group member 1:	No, I guess I just meant that I should not be alone with little kids.
Group leader:	What was it about your victims that turned you on?

Group member 1:	I don't know.
Group leader:	What do you mean you do not know?
Group member 1:	I guess their butts. I guess that I picked two people that were almost becoming teenagers, and I liked the way their butts looked.
Group leader:	What was it about them that made you want to offend them?
Group member 1:	I liked the way their little butts were round and juicy.
Group leader:	Okay, so you might want to stay away from children whom you feel like you might be attracted to their round, juicy behinds.
Group leader:	What else about your victims made them appealing?
Group member 1:	I don't know.
Group leader:	Did you pick them because they were younger and you did not think that they would tell on you?
Group member 1:	Yeah, I know that they would not tell on me.
Group leader:	So, maybe you should stay away from children that you think might be vulnerable?
Group member 1:	Yeah.
Group leader:	What might make them more vulnerable?
Group member 1:	I don't know.
Group member 2:	What about kids that are in a room alone without their parents?
Group member 1:	Yeah, I don't think I would do anything, but just so I can be sure and no will think anything, I should not be in the room alone with them.
Group leader:	Okay, so we have identified a couple of different things here that might make being around children a little safer. You have identified what it is about your victims that made you attracted to them and how you were able to have access to them. Now that you know that, you can make your plan around those issues.
Group member 1:	Okay.
Group leader:	Do you see how that is more concrete than "I am just not going to be around kids at all?" I would imagine that not being around kids would be impossible, whereas the things that we just talked about will help you to have a plan to be around children safely and supervised.

Question 5.3: Devise an open-ended question that could take the place for each leading or closed-ended question in the scenario above.

Construct questions so as to elicit strengths. One strategic use of language is the use of definitive (also called presuppositional) phrasing that conveys the expectation that change will occur. Words such as "when" and "will" are used, such as, "*When* you are better, what *will* you be doing?" Definitive phrasing is contrasted with possibility phrasing, marked by words, such as "*If*" and "*could/can*" (e.g., If you get better, what could you be doing?"). The latter phrasing implies doubt that the client can change. In an independent living group geared toward preparing older foster care youth to age out of the child welfare system, one of the group facilitators posed the question, "So can you think of things you can do to stay safe?" Group members met the question with silence. Instead the question can be phrased, "What things do you do to keep yourself safe?" This line of inquiry implies that the group members are already taking steps to ensure their safety and sets up a positive expectancy that they will have answers to share with the group.

Avoid the use of "why" questions as they can sound judgmental and accusatory ("Why did you do that?"). Additionally, "why" questions may produce rumination and intellectualizing, when in group one wants to elicit feelings, specific thoughts and behaviors, or resources. In general, use "what" and "how" questions because these open up the group members to more possibilities and resources.

One more pattern to guard against as a group leader is asking too many questions. In motivational interviewing, the general rule is that for every one question you ask, make three statements (Miller & Rollnick, 2002). The advantage of groups is that questions can be directed to the group rather than repeatedly to one group member ("Have others shared this experience?" "What do you think [group member] was feeling in this situation?").

Question 5.4: Note the use of "why" questions in the open-ended adult sex offender group scenario described in the previous chapter. What is your reaction to them?

ALLOWING THE GROUP TO HAVE OWNERSHIP

This section could also be titled, "Let the Group Do the Work." This can be quite a relief to beginning group workers. They do not have to be responsible for everything that happens in the group; they do not have to possess all the answers! These are methods to allow the group to "own" their group (Toseland & Rivas, 2009):

- Support members' communications with each other rather than addressing the leader.

    Example: As a group member reacts to Nicole's story about yet another break-up with her boyfriend, she addresses the leader. The leader could say to the group member, "I wonder if you could tell Nicole directly what you are thinking."

- Promote mutual sharing and aid.

    Example: In a parenting group, Pat talks about the difficulty of being able to discipline his children when they defy him. The group leader asks, "I wonder if anyone else in the room can relate to what Pat is going through with his children."

- Solicit members' input into how the group will proceed.

    Example: During check-in for a social phobia group, Greta becomes emotional talking about her week. The group leader asks, "I wonder if we should deal with Greta's feelings now or should we continue with the check-in and come back to her?"

- When the group leader is asked a question, it can be redirected back to the other members.

    Example: In a health education group for people with schizophrenia, the group leader asks what the members ate for lunch. Tom answers, "I didn't eat the cake. I ate the chicken and vegetables. Was that good?" In this case, the leader could ask the other group members, "What do you think of Tom's choices for lunch?"

- When two members or the leader and a member are at an impasse, the leader can open it up to the group.

    Example: As part of an addictions program in a prison setting, group members prepare a "life story" wherein they share the story of their addiction and read it aloud. One group member, Debra, has just related that she and her siblings switched off care of their children with each other during the summer time. Debra has said that she spent a lot of time using cocaine and shoplifting during one particular summer. Another group member, Vera raises her hand too.

    Vera: Well, I think they were enabling you. I think you need to look at that. I didn't have anyone to help me. I did it all by myself.

    Debra: That's the way my family works. We would trade off. I get all the kids for two weeks, then my one sister, then my other sister, then my brother, so it ended up that we all got almost the whole summer to ourselves. We still did get-togethers and if the kids wanted to come home, that was okay, but they liked going to all their cousins' houses. It was fun for them, and it was like a vacation for me and them.

    Vera: For you, huh? You didn't have to face reality, girl. You got to live in some fantasy world and didn't have to face motherhood like I did. I was here all by myself, no mother, sisters, nothing, not even a husband that was ever home, he was out partying. I think that your family just encouraged you to live a single person's lifestyle and you didn't face up or own up to your responsibilities, that just gave you more time to shoplift and drug it up.

In this scenario, Vera was becoming more insistent, whereas Debra didn't seem to think Vera's point had much relevance for her. Rather than continuing the interactional pattern between the two group members, the group leader could intercede and re-direct the focus to the group as a whole. As in, "What's the difference between people being enabling and people being supportive?"

Question 5.5: Refer again to the adolescent sex offender group scenario discussed on pages 63-64. In that scenario, how could the group leader get the other group members involved in the discussion?

Question 5.6: In the scenario, on pages 57-58, in the psychiatric hospital in which Harold kept inserting his opinion on the way Marcus felt toward his mother, how could the social worker have opened up the interaction to the rest of the group?

Read the following scenario and answer the question that follows:

This social skills group takes place at a middle school for youth who have been categorized as "emotionally disturbed" and is facilitated by a social worker and the social work intern. Group members consist of one boy, Brian, who has been diagnosed with Asperger's, Evelyn and Jill who have both been diagnosed with Anxiety Disorders. This group session adds a new member to the group, Diedre, a 12-year-old girl with Asperger's. The members, up until this point, are working on how to initiate contact with others and how to respond to overtures from others.

Leader:	Well, as I said we have a new student who is joining our group. Everyone, this is Diedre. Diedre, what are you doing this weekend?
Diedre:	Nothing.
Leader:	Nothing, or nothing you want to talk about?
Diedre:	Just nothing!

| Leader: | Okay, you don't have to talk about it if you don't want to, but we do have to talk to each other with respect. Let's take a few minutes because we have a new group member, and review so that we all can know and remember our rules for group. First, we always treat our group members with respect. What we say in group, we don't talk about outside of group, because this is a safe space to talk about— |

(Evelyn raises her hand.)

Leader:	Evelyn, is this something related to what we are talking about?
Evelyn:	Yes, um. We shouldn't talk about what happens in here because—
Diedre:	What? Your name is Evelyn? But that's a <u>girl's</u> name!
Evelyn:	I <u>am</u> a girl.
Diedre:	No, you're not.
Evelyn:	I understand that because my hair is short that sometimes people think that this might be a boy haircut, but I am a girl.
Diedre:	Are you sure?
Evelyn:	Yes.
Leader:	Diedre, you have asked that already. Now you heard her name is Evelyn, and that's a girl's name, and that should tell you she is a girl, and she's told you she is a girl.
Diedre:	But I thought he was a boy!
Leader:	Well, she is a girl. Now our other rules for group are—

(Diedre raises her hand.)

| Leader: | Yes, Diedre? |
| Diedre : | *(pointing at Jill)* What's wrong with <u>her</u>? |

(At everyone's attention turning to her, Jill's face crumples, and she begins to tear up.)

| Leader | Diedre, there is absolutely nothing wrong with Jill, and we have talked about how you need to respect people. |

(Jill is crying now.)

Leader:	Jill, are you—
Diedre:	Look! There is something wrong with her!
Leader:	Jill, was there something wrong?

(Jill shakes her head.)

| Leader: | Were you just bothered by Diedre's saying that? |

(Jill nods.)

| Leader: | Okay, Jill, why don't you and I step out of the room for a minute? |

(Jill and the leader leave as the student intern takes over.)

Question 5.7: How could the social work leader have gotten the group more involved in the work of the group?

An additional way to push members to take ownership is when they test the guideline that was set up about handling issues as a group. Individuals may contact you individually and voice a complaint about the group or make a suggestion. Your job is to refer the member back to the group: "You make an excellent point. Be sure to bring it up next time we meet so we can discuss it as a group." The member may insist that the issue is too sensitive. You must recognize that if a person takes the risk of bringing up a sensitive issue in group (e.g., "I'm trying to get what I can from the group, but it's hard when the rest of you are giggling and whispering all the time"), they are vulnerable to rejection or anger from other members. Therefore, you, as the group facilitator, have to be able to protect the individual group member; otherwise, the group member will feel unfairly exposed, and other group members will decide it is unsafe to show vulnerability in the future.

Protecting the group member involves first, complimenting the person for coming forward and expressing him or herself, emphasizing that it takes a lot of courage to do so. The group facilitator can then ask whether other people in group share the same concerns. If others do agree, the discussion can move forward from there. If there is no response, the group facilitator can suggest that the person brought up an important issue and might be speaking for other people, who at this time are unable to risk giving voice to their concerns. The facilitator can then ask what specific behaviors the group member would like to see from others.

FINDING COMMONALITIES AND MAKING LINKING STATEMENTS

An important way to help build group cohesion—the sense of community and togetherness within a group (Corey & Corey, 2006)—is to find the commonalities between group members' feelings and experiences. The leader may choose to remind the group as they begin to share feelings: "Our experiences may be different, but we all have feelings, and have all felt shame, guilt, doubt, sadness, anger. While we all have different paths and experiences that got us here, the one thing everyone shares in this room is that we are here now."

In addiction recovery groups, for example, there are many different types of people, but the clear commonality is the painful struggle with addiction and the feelings of helplessness and guilt that often accompany such a struggle. A member sharing about an experience may touch on feelings of guilt, giving the leader an opportunity to note how this feeling, while possibly precipitated by a different situation, sounds similar to the guilt described by another member. Or, the leader can bring in the other member by asking: "Does the feeling he describes with this experience sound familiar to what you shared last week?" Although these are different experiences, universal emotions are invoked.

Yet one more example involves how people feel about their parents. A 20-year-old male and a 50-year-old woman may both discover that they continue to seek approval from their parents. Although they may have different approval-seeking behaviors, they can come together around the pain related to not receiving the approval they both so clearly desire. When the leader emphasizes the communication, the members feel less alone, and see more similarities rather than differences, between themselves and others.

Group leaders will often make statements to link different group members' experiences. In the following example, the members of an inpatient substance abuse treatment group respond to the leader's question about times they were able to refrain from using drugs. The first group member talked about wanting to keep his job so he could make child support payments. The social work intern then enlarged upon his statements about caring for his child. See how the student intern linked his statements to the concerns of the rest of the group.

Social Work Intern:	Has anyone else not used for similar reasons?
Sue:	Yeah, I can relate. I have two kids and one that CPS already took because of my using. I can remember one time I was on the street and had my last bit of money. I was going to give it to the dope man, but something in me just stopped. I had a picture of my daughter in my mind, and I knew she needed food. So I went on home.
Social Work Intern:	So it sounds like for both of you, your children were big factors in stopping you from using on that occasion. How about the rest of you?
Robert:	I didn't use one time because my mom was in the hospital, and I knew if I used I would never go see her. The doctors said it was serious, and I didn't want her to die and never see her again. So I went to the hospital, and I was real glad I did.
Social Work Intern:	What about going to the hospital made you feel good?
Robert:	It was just seeing my mom's face when I walked in the door. She was really happy to see me. Now I did go out and use right after that, but not before.
Social Work Intern:	Can you see any common themes in what kept you all from using?
Susan:	Family members—kids, mom.
Social Work Intern:	What can we learn from that?
Susan:	That family is real important and people count on us.
Robert:	We're supposed to be responsible.
John:	It's important because they love us.
Social Work Intern:	So how might knowing that family members count on you and love you help you the next time you want to use?
John:	Just remembering their faces sometimes get me through.
Social Work Intern:	How about the rest of you? What do you think?
Susan:	Sometimes if I just concentrate real hard on thinking about my baby and how I really do want a better life for her, and I don't want her to go down the same path I went, sometimes that helps me.
Social Work Intern:	So it sounds like for all of you, a family member in need played a big part. John, your son needed child support. Susan, your daughter needed food. Robert, your mom needed to see you when she was sick. All of you said earlier that using drugs makes you feel like a loner, but you've all described people in your lives that really need you and love you. So maybe if we can work on building the relationships with the people that matter most to you, perhaps you can find ways to feel more connected and not so alone.
Group Members:	Yeah, that makes sense.

As this example illustrates, one important task of the group facilitator is to connect different members' experiences with each other to build group cohesiveness. In this way, people learn that others share their experiences and that they are not "crazy," "alone," or "different."

STRUCTURING GROUP MATERIAL

We have referred to the fact in Chapter 2 that social workers, depending on the population with whom they work and the setting where they are employed, will often lead structured groups, those that revolve around the provision of information and the use of activities that help group members learn about particular topics germane to their problem (Toseland & Rivas, 2009).

Many groups possess an emphasis on educational material; for instance, educational groups, psychoeducational groups, and treatment groups that are structured in nature, such as cognitive-behavioral groups, all have information to present. However, limit the delivery of lecture-type format; instead, present material in collaboration with clients (Carroll, 1998). We will discuss certain ways to do this below. Finally, in this section, we will discuss how to relate activities to the purpose of the group.

Providing Information in a Collaborative Way

Here, certain strategies for imparting information collaboratively will be outlined, illustrated with examples.

- Elicit group members' knowledge of information.

For example: In a group of non-offending mothers of children who have been sexually abused, mothers learn information about sexual abuse dynamics (Corcoran, 2003). One dynamic many of them have difficulty understanding is why their children did not come to them immediately once the abuse first occurred. In order to begin talking about this dynamic, the group facilitator first asks the mothers to come up with possible reasons why children do not always disclose abuse right away. Some of the reasons might be easier for mothers to list, and for others, the group facilitator prompts the group members for responses, asking deductive questions that ultimately result in the following list (Deblinger & Heflin, 1996):

1. Fear for the child's safety
2. Children don't want to get the offender in trouble
3. Fear of blame and punishment
4. Loyalty to perpetrator
5. Fear for the effect on the family
6. Shame and embarrassment
7. Confusion/helplessness

After the list is formulated, the group leader asks the group members their reactions to it.

Group member #1: I guess there's a lot of good reasons why children might keep the abuse a secret.

Group member #2: And what might make it even more confusing to kids is that a bunch of these reasons may all be happening at the same time.

Group leader: Very good point.

(The group leader then moves into information about how long it takes children to reveal sexual abuse, again beginning by eliciting group members' knowledge on that topic.)

Group leader:	Does anyone want to guess how long the research tells us it takes before a child will disclose sexual abuse?
Group member #3:	Sometimes not until they're adults. I didn't tell anyone that I was sexually abused by my father until all this came out.
Group leader:	Sometimes people don't talk about it until they are all grown up. Fortunately, there is now more attention to sexual abuse, so hopefully people won't wait as long. Despite all the awareness, though, children still delay telling an average of 1.5 years. If the offender is a family member, it is even longer: 2.6 years (Wolfe, 2006).

In this example, the facilitator asks the group members about their knowledge of sexual abuse, so they can be actively involved in the presentation. A second benefit is that the group leader might adjust a presentation according to the extent of member knowledge on a topic. Finally, when people have been given an opportunity to first reflect on what they know about a certain topic, they are then usually more receptive to information.

- Elicit group members' reactions to information

    For example: in a brain injury support group, the student intern led a session featuring depression. She began by discussing that depression was a common result of brain injury.

Intern:	The research shows that anywhere between 30 to 49% of people with brain injuries have depression. Today, we're going to talk about your experiences with depression. What's your reaction to these statistics?
John:	That seems too small of a number. What I have experienced is not just depression, but frustration that becomes anger that becomes depression. And sometimes I just can't handle it because I get so tired.
Pam:	Me, too, plus what worked to get rid of depression before the accident doesn't work any more. So I'm left trying new things with what seems like half of the original equipment.
Intern:	That's a very good point. The brain regulates your moods and emotions, but with the brain injury, this system is altered and one must find new strategies to address all of the anger, frustration, and fatigue that come with brain injury.

- Ask group members to describe information in their own words: *Note the following exchange in an open-ended educational health group, which is held weekly at a residential facility for people with schizophrenia.*

Social Work Intern:	Today we've been talking about calories. Let's review what we discussed. Can someone tell me what an empty calorie is?
Mary:	It's sodas, candy, pie, ice cream, candy and that sort of thing...like Snickers, M&Ms, Butterfingers, cookies, pies, Mars, Coke, Root Beer, ice cream, chocolate, hard candy, Ginger Ale, Pepsi, Mountain Dew—
Tom:	It's sugar. I don't eat a lot of sugar.
Social Work Intern:	Exactly, empty calories are basically sugary foods that don't have much nutritional value. People tend to use them for a source of quick energy. But what happens then?

Sally:	What comes up, must come down.
Social Work Intern:	Yes, your blood sugar goes up, then comes crashing down, making you feel worse than you did in the first place.

- Have group members apply information to their own experience:

Returning to the example of the health group, the intern says, "Let's discuss what you all had for lunch today. Were there any empty calories served?"

Henry:	We had cake.
Tom:	I didn't eat the cake. I ate the chicken and vegetables.

Another group member explains that the cake was an example of empty calories. In this way, the group members are engaged in the information that is being provided and make it applicable to their own lives.

Structuring Activities

As the group leader, provide succinct, yet clear directions on how to complete an activity. For example, in the psychoeducational group for mothers of sexual abuse victims, the group leader, after discussing information on "I" messages, said, "In order to get some practice on using 'I' messages, I want each of you to think about a person in your life with whom you are having some difficulty." She paused here, scanning the group to see that she had everyone's attention and that they understood her so far. She allowed a little time for reaction as some members laughed or nodded, recalling a particular conflict they were having. Here, she continued, "You each have a sheet of paper before you. I want you to write an 'I' message to that person, using the format we have talked about." Here she indicated a large poster board sheet tacked to the front of the room in which the elements of "I" messages were presented. "After you have some time to do that, we will go around and share our 'I' statements, and I will write them on this poster board. Does everyone understand what we're doing? Let me answer any questions you have."

As this example illustrates, the group leader provides instructions on the activity and how it relates to the information that has been provided. After the activity has been completed, the group leader can process with the members what they learned from the activity. Such a discussion can relate the activity to the purpose of the session.

I realized the importance of such a rationale when I was leading the group for adolescents involved in the criminal justice system. I worried initially that if I spent too much time talking, I would lose the boys' attention. One time, I assigned the boys a collage activity representing their lives as they wanted them to be after they had worked to free themselves from illegal activity. The members were compliant, but as one boy cut and glued, he commented, "Why are we doing this, just to keep busy?" I had to laugh at myself, because he had pinpointed my neglect to make clear to him and the other group members the link between the goal of the group and the activity. I certainly didn't want them to think I was just having them do busywork rather than activities that would have value to them.

REINFORCING DESIRABLE GROUP BEHAVIORS

The group leader must be vigilant for behaviors that he or she would like to reinforce in group members, such as:

- Sharing feelings (e.g., "I know that was difficult stuff to get into, LaShawn, but you were able to talk about your own reactions instead of being angry at someone else. That shows a lot of progress on your part.")

- Asking for specific feedback (e.g., "Did you see how Jenny asked for the group's reaction about how she managed the conflict with her sister? She didn't just tell the story, leaving us to wonder, she told us what she needed."

- Being open to hearing feedback (e.g., "Tarryn, I'm sure some of the feedback you were getting about how you come off to others was difficult to hear, but you listened very well to what your fellow group members had to say.")

- Being willing to try out new ways to approach problems (e.g., "I'm hearing that it felt very awkward to talk about your feelings with your girlfriend rather than yelling at her, but it's wonderful that you were willing to do something different this time when you found yourself getting mad.")

- Reflecting other members' feelings (e.g., "That's great, Trish, rather than telling Paul what he should do, you were able to reflect back what he was feeling when he saw his dad.")

- Keeping people on track when they seem to drift into tangential speech (e.g., "Thank you, Lee, for getting the group back on focus.")

- Pointing out strengths and giving positive feedback (e.g., "Robert, I'm impressed how you're able to see the good in other people.")

Not only do you benefit members by complimenting them, you also let the group know what behaviors you want in group and model for them how to find strengths in others.

De Jong et al. (2008) suggests a form of complimenting called "indirect complimenting" in which positive traits and behaviors are implied. Examples of indirect complimenting include: "How were you able to do that?" "How did you figure that out?" These questions push the client to figure out the resources they used to achieve success.

SUMMARY

This chapter has focused on some of the basic skills social workers need to demonstrate when they lead groups. Many of these skills, such as showing empathy and asking questions will be familiar to the reader because they are also shown when working with clients individually. However, others of these, such as making linking statements to join members of the group together and to create cohesiveness, and letting the group take ownership are specific to group work. In the next chapter, we will turn to more advanced group work skills.

Chapter 6
Advanced Leadership Skills

This chapter will focus on group leadership skills that the beginning social work leader might find somewhat challenging. These include: 1) asking members to be specific and concrete; 2) inviting members to talk about their feelings and reactions; 3) ensuring that group members give appropriate feedback; 4) maintaining the focus in the group; 5) providing advice; 6) attending to the here and now; and 7) appropriate self-disclosure as a leader.

ASKING MEMBERS TO BE SPECIFIC AND CONCRETE

As we have discussed when formulating guidelines for group behavior, some people are more comfortable talking in generalities about "you" or "they" when they are talking about themselves. A guiding principle in therapeutic situations is to stop people when they talk about "you," and ask them to whom they are referring. This will get them to speak about themselves more personally. In addition, people tend to describe situations or experiences in general terms ("My boss has it in for me"), but in order to get more in-depth, they have to describe specific circumstances and explore what happened. Questions such as the following can be asked:

- When you talk about "people doing bad things," can you tell me what you mean by that?
- Can you give a specific example?
- Can you explain what happened in this instance?

This example relates to the process group for adolescents that was run in a residential treatment program (see question 3.1). After the initial railing about the way the group would be run, the teens began to set the course for the particular group session.

Group member 1:	Okay, the topic today is going to be teen relationships. How do you know if a person is right for you?
Group member 2:	Well, I think that boys are busters[1].
Group member 3:	Sometimes you just sense it and that's when you know it is wrong.
Group member 4:	You can tell by the way a person acts around you. You can tell if they just flirt with you or if they are flirting with everyone else too.
Group leader:	I am interested to know how is it that you can tell if they are being real or just faking it?
Group member 2:	You need to talk to them on the phone and get to know them that way.
Group member 4:	I will ask their friends if they are being real with you.
Group member 2:	They're fake if they act different around you when it's just you than they act towards you when there are other people around.

---

[1] "Buster" means fake.

Group member 1: This person has to be someone you can consider getting close to, someone sensitive to your needs, someone you can take the next step with.

Group member 2: You can give them a little truth about yourself and see what they do with it.

Group member 4: I give them a little of my life story.

Group Leader: How would telling your life story help you to see if they are real or fake?

Group member 4: Well, once they find out I'm in foster care if they pull away and get freaked out, then I'll know they are fake. But if they try to understand and talk to me, then they are real.

Group member 2: What would you do if your boy or girlfriend was cheating on you?

Group member 3: I'd try to set him up so that I could catch him in the act.

In this example, after the first group member brought up, "How do you know if a person is right for you?" the conversation from there remains on a fairly superficial and general level. To deepen the dialogue, the group facilitator could ask if the initial group member was considering a specific situation or an actual relationship that spurred his question. The exploration of the feelings and experiences associated with a concrete situation has much to teach about abstract questions, such as "How do you know if a person is right for you?"

The following scenario involves an open-ended support group for mothers in recovery (all members have both a substance use disorder and a mental health disorder). For now, we will ignore the tendency of client #2 to try to take over the group (see Chapter 13) and will focus on how to get the group members to talk in more concrete terms about their concerns. How would you do this as the group leader? (Write your response in the area provided following this scenario.)

Leader: Who would like to start?

Client 1: Well, I just reconnected with my kids this weekend for the first time in months. I mean I had them at my house. They was gettin' on my nerves. I just felt so overwhelmed. I was like "am I ready for this?" I'm just not sure I am ready to be back with them again.

Leader: So you have been apart from your children and you are just starting to get used to them again?

Client 1: Yeah. We had a sleepover. All four of them were there and we made popcorn and watched a movie. It was fun but they were also gettin' on my nerves. I was starting to feel overwhelmed.

Client 2: You know, Client 1, you're doing a good job. Having kids can be stressful for anyone but especially because you are just getting back with them and reestablishing your relationships. Plus, you are going through your own stuff, you know? You've been clean now for what, 60 days? That's tough, you know? But you just have to take it a day at a time. When I'm with my two kids I get stressed out. They work on me and get on my nerves. But I have to remember myself and my own needs too, you know?

Client 1 *(nods):* Yes, I still focus on myself, too.

Client 3: I'm trying to get my daughter back. I don't have custody of her no more. She will be 18 soon though. I'm hoping I can get her back.

Leader: Let's focus on what Client 2—

Client 2: Client 3, you have a tough situation, you know? I don't know what it's like to have custody taken from me but it must be very hard, you know? You have to remember that you have an illness, though, and your needs are important, too. I think if you just keep working on yourself and your own issues you will be able to get your daughter back. That's what I did in my situation. I just worked on myself, and I keep working on myself everyday and now things are getting easier with my kids.

Leader: Client 2, I would like to hear what Client 3 thinks—

Client 2: And if you just stay on task and keep focusing on yourself, that's the only way you will get your own issues resolved so that you can reunite with your daughter again. You know? Are you taking your medication, Client 4? You know it's important to keep taking your meds so you can keep your illness under control, right? If we don't all keep following with our own treatment, then we are going to keep having difficulty with our relationships with our kids.

Leader: I would like to go to Client 1 for a minute—

Question 6.1: How would you do this as the group leader?

Read the following scenario involving a psychoeducational group for people who have been diagnosed with depression. The group meets in a crisis care residential facility where all members have been staying for the past few days. The topic for the session is medication management.

Gina: You know, I take these meds and I just don't feel like myself.

Group leader: Yes, medications do affect people in ways that may seem highly unusual to the person who is taking them.

Kim : *(responding to Gina)* Yeah, I used to be so much skinnier, look at me, I've gained 20 pounds and I just don't feel attractive like I used to.

Group leader: Does anyone relate to how Gina and Kim feel about the effects of their medications?

Michelle : *(after about 20 seconds of silence)* Well, for me being on these antidepressants has made life pretty unpredictable. I don't know how I'll feel when I wake up in the morning.

Group leader: So the medication seems to affect your self-concept?

Stephanie: Yes, I feel like a different person when I'm taking my meds.

Group leader: So, you too feel like the medication changes who you are.

Question 6.2: After reading the scenario, what is the group leader is attempting to do after people speak? How could the group leader go deeper with people's concerns?

INVITING MEMBERS TO TALK ABOUT THEIR FEELINGS AND REACTIONS

One of the ways that people become vulnerable in group, share of themselves authentically, and take ownership of their own reactions is to talk about their feelings. Although there is a nuanced language for feelings, I like to keep it simple when I'm working with clients and talk about the main four: "happy," "sad," "scared," and "mad." Often, the group leader will ask members directly, "How are you feeling right now as you talk about this?" or reflect upon what they seem to be feeling, "I notice that you seem to be swallowing back tears of sadness as you talk."

There are some groups in which anger is a predominant theme, such as anger management and domestic violence intervention, conduct disorder treatment, and so forth. In such groups, members will easily admit feelings of anger and groups can stay focused on this emotion. However, other emotions often underlie the anger, such as sadness and fear. Therefore, in such groups, there could be a rule set up that people can talk about any other emotion but anger. Group members with such problems are often using anger defensively. By removing this possibility, you force them to get in touch with other feeling states. Many times, for example, anger is used in place of fear or hurt.

Social workers and other mental health and social service professionals often believe that people need to talk about their feelings in group about the difficult circumstances they have been through. There are some people in groups who are less likely to go along with this plan, however—for instance, adolescent and young men with conduct problems, especially when they attend open-ended groups in which participation is time limited. These group members may resist talking about feelings and become uncooperative or uncommunicative instead. Rather than getting into a struggle with clients about what they "should be dealing with" and pushing them into a direction they may find intrusive and irrelevant, coping questions are suggested. These imply that the client has shown resilience in surviving difficult life circumstances, and help clients figure out what qualities, resources, and supports were used (De Jong et al., 2008). Coping questions involve the following:

- "How have you coped with the problem?"

- "How do you manage? How do you have the strength to go on?"
- "This has been a very difficult problem for you. How have you managed to keep things from getting even worse?"
- "What do you tell yourself to keep going?"
- "What do you say to yourself to keep your sanity and hope when things are really hard?"

Question 6.3: In the adult sex offender group discussed previously (page 62), how would you ask coping questions? How might the featured group member have responded to them?

An additional opportunity for group members to share their feelings is when they blame or criticize others in the group. Often, when people experience painful feelings, they are more comfortable talking about someone other than themselves. Group leaders must be alert to this tendency and refocus the discussion to personal experiences: "What are you feeling right now?"

The excerpt involves an open-ended group called "Relationship Skills" that takes place at a day treatment program for people with chronic mental illness. Group members are completing a worksheet identifying problem behaviors.

Client #1:	What does the word super-dependence mean? Isn't it good to depend on others? It's not healthy to do everything on your own.
Social Work Intern:	You're right. It's definitely beneficial to rely on others for support. Super-dependency is being overly dependent on someone, not being able to do things for yourself.
Client #1:	Well, I depend on my husband for everything. We've been together for twenty years, and he does a lot for me.
Client #2:	It's a sign of weakness to depend on others too much. I am at a point in my life where I only depend on myself. I am the only one I can trust.
Client #1:	Are you saying there is something wrong with me because I depend on my husband a lot? There's nothing wrong with that. Is there, Social Work Intern?
Social Work Intern:	Being able to depend on your spouse is an important part of marriage. It's when you become unable to do things for yourself that the dependency becomes problematic. It is also unhealthy to isolate yourself, and not be able to rely on anyone at all.
Client #2:	I think anyone who relies on anyone else is pathetic. It is sick the way some people use their mates for money and other things. I will never make the mistake of marrying again. Worst thing I've ever done.

Social Work Intern: Client #2, you have some very strong opinions about dependency in quality relationships. What would you like to talk more about with the group?

Client #2: Nothing. It's really no one else's business about my failed marriage. It's just pathetic, though, how some people have to rely on others for everything. It's disgusting really.

Client #1: Who do you think you are? Are you calling me pathetic? My husband and I have been together for a long time. Just because he gives me money doesn't mean I'm using him. And it doesn't mean I'm super-dependent. I can't believe you have the nerve to say that about me--in front of my face, too. You white girls have no idea what it is like to be a black woman in this city. You just have no idea.

Client #2: Me being white has nothing to do with being too dependent on people. I have made the choice to only depend on myself. That is my personal choice, and I have a right to it. Just like you're free to keep your relationship with your husband as it is. It is not my business to tell you that things should change. It's your problem, not—

Social Work Intern: Okay, okay, I understand that you both have very important things to add to the group discussion, but I'm going to have to ask you to keep your comments to yourself, if you can't respect what others are saying. In order to keep this group a safe place for everyone to voice their ideas and opinions we need to make sure everyone's views are heard and respected. That does not mean you have to agree with them—just that you respect them.

Client #1: How am I supposed to respect someone who is insulting me in front of my face? I can't believe this B**H! Do you know what I've gone through to get my marriage to where it is today? Did you know he used to hit me? Did you know that? Did you know we used to use together? We'd use and then he'd beat me up. And he has a baby with someone else! Do you know how close to using again I was when I heard that? I've been clean for three months now, and I've been coming here to help me with things. You have no idea how things are for me.

Client #2: I know that you are a pathetic woman if you really think your husband loves you. He's probably cheating on you because he knows how you need him for everything

Social Work Intern: Ladies, there's a better way to handle this. It is inappropriate and absolutely disrespectful to—

Client #1: Whatever! Screw all of you! F*** this place! I'm getting the hell out of here.

(Leaves and slams the door behind her)

Client #2: I don't know what her problem is. Sometimes the truth hurts. She just needs to—

Social Work Intern: Please, Client #2. This is not the time to bad mouth Client #1. We can talk about what happened at the break, but right now in front of the rest of the group is not the time.

Client #2: Fine, I don't have anything else to say anyway.

She folds her arms across her chest and slumps down in her seat for the remainder of group.

The student intern in this situation must be given credit for tolerating a difficult and uncomfortable situation. She tried to get the group member who was railing about dependence being "pathetic" to talk about her own experiences by saying, "Client #2, you have some very strong opinions about dependency in quality relationships. What would you like to talk more about with the group?" Unfortunately, the group member rejected this gambit and the conflict escalated. When it did, the leader reminded the group members about the necessity of maintaining respect for each other.

Perhaps the group member would have responded to a simpler and more direct question, "What are you feeling right now?" If she could start talking about hurt over a previous relationship betrayal , the focus would then be on her, rather than the conflict with the other group member.

Question 6.4: Recall the anger management session on "compassion" (see pages 32-33). How would you approach this interaction in the group after reading the previous material?

ENSURING THAT GROUP MEMBERS GIVE APPROPRIATE FEEDBACK

Following from the above discussion, a valuable aspect of the group process is that people share their reactions towards each other. In this way, the recipient can learn more about how he or she relates to others, and the giver of feedback can learn about how to communicate assertively.

The leader's responsibility is to teach people to give feedback in a way that is both honest and authentic *and* is sensitive to the other person's feelings. One important way to structure feedback is to suggest that the speaker talk from a personal position using an "I" message. Further, the person should speak in specific terms about a person's behavior rather than making characterological references (e.g., "You're mean."). Note this example of feedback to a group member that encapsulates this structure: "When you say you don't care about having a relationship in your life, I don't believe you because otherwise why would you keep coming to this group? I think you should admit that you want a relationship and then you might be more open toward it. When you keep saying that, it makes me not want to have a relationship with you, and you might be turning other people off, too."

When feedback is vague or given inappropriately, the leader can also invite group participation: "What do others hear in this message?" or "Are there any other ways this could have been said?" Group leaders can also *reframe* an inappropriate reaction (more on reframing will be offered in Chapter 11). For example, in a group for women who were involved in intimate partner violence, one of the members related that she had returned to her violent husband. One of the other members responded, "Are you crazy? You know he's going to end up killing you!" The group leader, in this situation, said to the woman who had first spoken, "I think what she's trying to say is that she is worried about you."

In addition to monitoring the content of the feedback, the leader must also attend to the *amount* of feedback any one person receives. Not uncommonly in groups, people go on "the attack" with a member who is vulnerable. The group leader might have to intervene in such a circumstance: "Let's hold off for now and check in with [the recipient of the feedback] and see how you're feeling and your reaction to what you heard people say."

MAINTAINING THE FOCUS IN THE GROUP

Sometimes group conversations may veer off in tangential or unproductive channels. This happens for a variety of reasons. Some people tend to be storytellers and monopolizers of the group's time, wanting a lot of attention on themselves and finding it difficult to share group time. This particular challenge will be discussed in Chapter 13. Other reasons for tangents is that the group members do not want to deal with uncomfortable material, and by keeping the group off-focus they do not have to face the hard work of confronting material directly. By being tangential, people might also succeed in keeping the group at a superficial level rather than getting into more depth. People sometimes are scared to risk the authentic sharing that depth entails and are afraid of getting hurt or rejected. Before they can risk, they may need to feel that sufficient safety exists in the group.

There are many options for dealing with tangents that group members take (for individuals with these behaviors, see Chapter 13):

- Redirect the tangent.

    For example, in the teen "self-esteem" group at the inpatient hospital unit, one of the group members mentioned a family meeting that had taken place the day before and complained about a therapist, who made statements in family meetings that she didn't make at other times. Other group members shared their experiences about her doing the same thing. In this case, the group leader allowed the members a few minutes to speak. When each member had the opportunity to speak once, and the discussion seemed to be gaining steam, she redirected the group, by saying, "We aren't here to process about the therapist and have a group about her. Let's get back to our topic."

- Ask the group if the tangent is an avenue worth pursuing.

    For example, in the teen group perhaps the members could be asked if they want to turn their attention on communicating assertively with adults.

- If a pattern of storytelling emerges in the group, the group leader can point out this pattern and ask the group members both what they are getting out of this (they don't have to face painful subjects, they protect against change) and what they may potentially lose (i.e., is the group going to be able to meet its goals?). When presented with a cost-benefit analysis, the group members can be challenged to decide if they want to do something about this pattern.

- If the group leader senses that the group may have veered off after sensitive or deep work was being discussed, she might stop and ask for group members' observations of the transaction.

In the example of the teen group, perhaps before the group member began criticizing the family therapist, she was getting into some important family work. If this was the case, the leader could draw the group members' attention to this point. We will talk more about process observations in the next section.

Question 6.5: Recall the scenario of the teen group in the residential treatment center (see page 22). What technique did she use to try to get the group back on track? What other techniques from the above list might she have tried?

PROVIDING ADVICE

As discussed, people in groups (and in all social situations) easily move into advice-giving mode, and the group leader must to ensure that people's feelings and experiences are processed first: "Before we tell Denise what we think she should do, let's hear more about the struggle she's having with her elderly mother." Recall the example of Nicole in Chapter 4 and how group members' attempts to solve her problems only increased her feelings of pain.

At the same time, members often seek out groups because they want to know what to do about certain situations or problems and may want to know about what has been helpful for others. Before the group leader enters into advice-giving, here are some guidelines to follow:

1. Make sure that the person's feelings and situation have been understood and validated.

2. Ask other group members what they know or what has worked for them. They are less likely to share their ideas if the group leader speaks first on the topic, so allow group members an opportunity to share (Toseland & Rivas, 2009).

3. Be tentative about giving advice: "I think I understand your perspective on this. I wonder if it would be okay for me to tell you a few things that occur to me as I listen to you, which you might want to consider" (Miller & Rollnick, 2002).

Chapter 12 will cover how to teach group members about the problem-solving process, which can channel people's advice-giving tendencies.

ATTENDING TO THE HERE AND NOW

The most valuable aspect of groups according to Yalom (2005) is that one can work on interpersonal functioning on a here and now basis. For example, an open-ended support group for men with serious mental illness focused a session on "men and emotions." A leader and a social work intern facilitated this group.

Leader: Hello, how's everyone doing this morning? Today we're going to talk about men and emotions.

Jeff: You mean like crying? Is it okay for men to cry?

Leader: Good question, Jeff. What do you think?

Jeff: I cried when Mary died. She committed suicide. I'm mad at her. Do you think she's going to hell?

(Mary was Jeff's best friend. She had died by suicide about two weeks prior to this group session.)

SW Intern: You seem very sad about your friend's death, and you miss her. You're also angry she took her own life.

Jeff: Yeah.

Diego: I think it's hard for men to show their emotions. They are supposed to be strong, you know? Women expect too much of men. They want us to be strong, you know? We're supposed to take care of them, give them money, but we don't get much in return.

Leader: So you're saying that women have an image of men being strong, non-emotional providers. Can someone tell us where we get this image of males being stoic providers from?

Steve: The movies. James Bond.

Jeff: *(with a bright affect)* I like James Bond. Did you see that one called...um...I don't know, but it was good. *(Affect suddenly darkens.)* I'm mad at Mary. Why did she do that? *(Slumps down in his seat.)*

Diego: Was she a Christian?

Jeff: She went to church. I don't think she's going to hell.

(Alex mutters something unintelligible.)

Leader: What was that, Alex?

Alex: I'm leaving here. I have a big house. You can't make me stay.

SW Intern: *(deciding to ignore Alex)* Diego, your religion is very important to you.

Diego: Yeah, suicide is a sin.

Jeff: What are you saying—that Mary's going to hell?

Diego: Suicide is a sin.

Jeff: What? Stop saying that, Diego. You're upsetting me.

Diego: It's a fact, man. The Bible says that if we kill ourselves, we're going to hell.

Jeff: *(starts crying)* Why are you saying that? Mary was my best friend!

Leader: Hey, guys, it's all right. We can have different religious beliefs. Jeff, what's important is what you think about Mary.

Jeff: You mean if I think she's not going to hell, she isn't?

SW Intern: Jeff, what do you believe?

Jeff *(smiling)*: Mary was a good person. She wouldn't hurt a flea. I don't think she's going to hell. She's an angel. Sometimes I see her with wings and a gold circle over her head. She's smiling at me.

SW Intern: Jeff, Mary meant a lot to you. It's good that you have fond memories of her that you carry around with you.

At that point, the group went in a different direction, talking about movies that promoted stereotypes of men.

Since the theme of the group was "men and emotions," the leaders could have stayed with the emotions Jeff was sharing and the group members' reactions to him. Instead, they turned the group's attention away from the present moment and to the past when the leader asked where group members received their messages about men being "strong," which eventually led to a discussion about movies. After Diego said, "I think it's hard for men to show their emotions. They are supposed to be strong, you know? Women expect too much of men. They want us to be strong, you know? We're supposed to take care of them, give them money, but we don't get much in return," the leader could have asked, "Diego, what are you picking up on how Jeff is feeling right now?" We will continue here with a hypothetical response.

Diego: Well, suicide is a sin.

Leader: What does Jeff seem to be feeling? Mad, sad, scared?

Diego: Sad.

Leader: Could you tell him that?

Diego: Jeff, you seem really sad.

Jeff: *(nods and start to tear up)* Why did she have to do that?

(The men seem uncomfortable and Alex mutters a statement that is unrelated to the group discussion.)

Leader *(to everyone)*: What are you all feeling as Jeff shoes his sadness?

Diego: I don't like it. She shouldn't have done that to him.

Leader: Diego, how are you feeling? Mad, sad, scared--

Diego: I feel mad at his friend.

Leader: How do you feel towards Jeff?

Diego: Like he must feel like he wants to run out of the room.

Leader: So you're embarrassed to see him upset? Embarrassment is a type of fear. What are you scared of?

Diego: That he's going to break down.

Leader: Can you tell him that?

Diego: I'm afraid you're going to break down, man.

Jeff: I'm okay. I'm not going to kill myself, if that's what you mean. I wouldn't do what she did to other people.

This type of conversation could take the group members to a deeper level about the experience of showing emotion as men as their feelings are explored and reflected.

After the dialogue has played itself out, which may bring the group to the end of the session, the leader could bringing back the theme of the group, "How does what we have been talking about relate to men and emotions?"

Part of working with the "here and now" is that the group leader stays attuned to the interactions and patterns in the group, focusing not on what the group was talking about (its content), but instead on its patterns of communication (its process). Focusing on process might be particularly important if a troublesome interaction pattern emerges in the group. See example of Nicole (page 59), and the teen group that got waylaid when the leader left the room, leaving the intern alone to cope (see question 6.5).

APPROPRIATE SELF-DISCLOSURE AS A LEADER

We will talk in Chapter 14 about managing challenging group moments, which include members asking leaders to disclose inappropriate personal information about themselves, but in this section, we will start with Yalom's (1985) general principle for self-disclosure. He reminds us that the main purpose of a group is to discuss "here and now" feelings. Therefore, in service of this goal, group leaders can make statements about their reactions to material being shared by group members. For instance, in the women's process group, the group leader shared, "Nicole, sometimes I feel a lot of responsibility for relieving you of how badly you feel, and I sense that you're disappointed with my efforts." This type of self-disclosure models the sharing of authentic feedback and risk-taking (Yalom, 1985).

SUMMARY

This chapter has covered skills that beginning group leaders might find more challenging to master. The examples and exercises have been placed so that readers can practice with different situations before they actually arise in a group setting and hopefully the presented scenarios will also stimulate further discussion and role plays in your classroom. Additionally, Chapters 13 and 14 will go into other potentially difficult situations group leaders may encounter.

Chapter 7
Stages of Group Development

With Elizabeth Blankespoor and Shane Fagan

Although many group work texts present the stages of group development early in the text, we have not discussed them until now. Why? Because many of the groups social workers lead do not proceed through the stages, due to the short-term and open-ended nature of many groups (e.g., as in acute inpatient units) in current practice. As we have noted, open-ended groups may develop through stages *if* a central core group of members participate on a regular basis.

Various group work writers present different stages of group development, and Toseland and Rivas (2009) do an excellent review. Before we give a general outline of these phases, one must note the absence of evidence supporting any particular order of the stages or of any clear demarcation of one stage from the other. (Yalom, 2005).

BEGINNING STAGE

In the beginning stage of group, members are often unsure of what is expected of them. They have uncertainties about whether they belong in the group and whether they may be helped in this way. They may feel nervous about revealing personal information and being vulnerable to others whom they do not know. These typical anxieties add to the member's specific concerns related to the problem that has brought them to group.

Leaders, as well, struggle with their own uncertainties and fear. "The leaders may wonder what the group will be like, whether they will be able to deal effectively with what comes up, and whether they will be able to bring a group of strangers together in such a way that the trust necessary for effective work is created" (Corey et al., 1992, p. 59). Leaders can use their own fears to remind them of what group members experience as they begin group. As we will discuss beginning groups in great detail (see Chapter 8), we will not go into the topic here.

MIDDLE STAGE

In the middle stage of group, there is an initial period of conflict, challenge, and adjustment as group members work out their relationships with each other and with the group leader (Toseland & Rivas, 2009; Yalom, 2005). These behaviors play out as members are determining the safety level of the group (Corey et al., 1992) and are seeking ownership of the group (Toseland & Rivas, 2009). During this phase, the group leader must manage conflict between members and perhaps even challenges to his or her own leadership (see Chapter 14). Cohesion and engagement in the group process ensue, and the therapeutic factors intrinsic to group work (see Chapter 1) become available to group members as they experience the "working" stage of the group (Corey et al., 1992).

The following excerpt shows the middle-stage (the 7th session) of a 12-week social phobia treatment group.

Social Worker:	Good morning! Let's get right down to business by doing our weekly "check in." Remember to limit yourselves to no more than three minutes each. Who would like to start?
Lori:	*(after about a 30 second pause)* Okay, if no one else wants to go, I might as well get this over with. My goal as you know is to start dating. Well, as I told everyone last session, I was supposed to have a "blind date" this past Saturday night with a guy named Jim. My sister knew him, and she pretty much arranged the whole thing. He called me Thursday night, according to my sister, to introduce himself, ask me what I wanted to do, and work out when and where to meet. As soon as the phone rang--I had an idea he was going to call that night--I started having heart palpitations and my hands and pits dripped with sweat. I saw on the caller ID that it was him, and I totally froze. I couldn't answer it! Oh my god, I'm getting all nervous again just thinking about it. *(reddens, shifts in chair)* Here I want to date when I can't even handle talking on the frigging phone! *(starting to sob)* I'm an absolute freak!! What's wrong with me?! *(sobbing harder)* I'll never get over this phobia!!
Janet:	*(patting her on the back)* Oh, Lori, it's okay. There's nothing wrong with you--we've all been there. You'll be dating in no time at all.
Lane:	*(to Janet)* What do you mean it's <u>okay</u>? Lori really looks okay, doesn't she? That's what you call okay?!! And why on earth are you telling her she'll "be <u>dating</u> in no time at all"? Want to lend me your crystal ball sometime?
Social Worker:	I'm going to interrupt you here. The group has a decision to make. Do you want to spend more time with Lori's issue now and continue with check-in later or get back to check-in and come back to Lori later?
John:	In light of Lori's distress, I think we should stay with this and if we have time later we can try to finish our check-in.
Lane:	I totally agree.
Janet:	I completely agree too. *(to Lori)* What can we do to make you feel better, honey?
Lori:	Nothing! *(no longer sobbing)* I just have to resign myself to the fact that no amount of therapy, no amount of group work, absolutely nothing is going to change the way I am—which is a pitiful, nervous, pathetic wreck.
Social Worker:	I wonder if the rest of you see Lori as a "pitiful, nervous, pathetic wreck"?
John:	No way! Lori, we're all here to overcome various aspects of our social phobias--so we all have that much in common. Over the past six weeks, we've all started to open up more in the group. One thing that I really admire—actually <u>envy</u>—is your sense of humor. You have added much needed humor on a number of occasions. I like you a lot and am happy that you're part of this group. I just wonder if you're biting off too much right now. What if you broke your goal of dating down into more manageable steps?
Lori:	Thanks, John. I don't see though how I can break something so simple into anything simpler—if that's even a word. *(smiles)*
Lane:	Anything "simpler"? You're just trying to do the most difficult thing known to mankind—dating! It's hard for anyone, much less for people who have social phobias. I'll never get divorced just because I'll never subject myself to that hellacious social ritual again—it was absolute <u>torture</u>! But I think you can break it down. How about if you spend more time with your sister and a couple of her friends? What if she even asked Jim to join your little group for lunch or drinks when you feel more comfortable about it? Avoid the intense one-on-one "dating" thing until you've built up a little more social confidence.

Richard: I think that's a really good idea, Lane. Another idea that I have is for <u>you</u>, Lori, to do the inviting. I think you might feel more empowered that way—even if it's just inviting your sister and one other friend. You could invite them to meet at your house for a drink before going to dinner or a movie, for instance. You could gradually increase the number of people you invite until you're actually hosting parties! I can see you doing that—start small and within your comfort zone and slowly push back the walls of that zone. At some point you might want to include Jim or some other guy you're interested in. It won't be a great big scary "date," and you'll already know that you're good at having people over to your house, which should ease the nervousness. And let me add that I too find you anything but a "pitiful, nervous, pathetic wreck." You're such a kind and genuine person, I'm very happy that I've gotten to know you.

Social Worker: Lori, you've just received some positive feedback from fellow group members and some interesting suggestions on how you might want to break down your goal of "dating." How do you feel about what you've heard?

Lori: I feel better hearing how supportive you all are—even if I have a hard time actually <u>believing</u> the nice things you've said about me. I'm just so down on myself, and I <u>still</u> feel like a total nut case. But I like the suggestions of taking smaller steps on the way to dating. Despite what I said, I don't want to give up on this group work. I really feel like we've become one big family, and if I can't make changes here, with all of you supporting me, I don't see how I'll ever make them. I think you're right—in order to get to my "ultimate" goal, I'll need—excuse me, I WANT to do it via much less threatening short-term and mid-term goals. My short-term goal will be to go over to my sister's house this weekend and tell her about my new plan. I have to give my mid-term goal some thought, but I'll let you know what it is next week.

Lane: You go, girl!!

Social Worker: Lori, you're coming from a much stronger place now than when you walked in here today. We'll be interested in hearing what you choose as your mid-term goal next week. Now before we return to our "check in," I think it's important to look at the interaction that took place between Janet and Lane a little while ago. Lane, you had a strong reaction to what Janet said. While keeping in mind our guidelines of "mutual respect," could you tell us what this strong reaction was all about?

Lane: I'd be happy to. She frustrates the hell—sorry, sorry—out of me with her "oh everything will always be wonderful" garbage.

Social Worker: She is sitting right here. Without using any offensive language, how about looking at her and telling her yourself how you feel?

Lane: Janet, I'm sure you probably mean well, but I sure don't feel like I'm seeing or hearing the <u>real</u> you. You're always trying to make everyone happy, and you bend over backwards trying to avoid any kind of confrontation between any group members. You seem to operate on this ultra superficial—but admittedly very sweet—level. I don't know; it just doesn't seem like you're really invested in this group. It's like what do you honestly feel below that sugar coating?

Janet: Well, I'm very sorry that you can't manage to accept me the way I am. This is the real me. *(looking at social worker)* Am I supposed to apologize for being myself?

John: I have to admit, Janet, that I don't feel like I know you at all either. You seem very sweet, but there has to be more to you than that. You wouldn't be here if there wasn't.

Social Worker: Janet, would you remind the group of your personal goal?

Janet: My goal is to make and maintain friendships with three people. I haven't had any real friends since elementary school because I'm so painfully shy.

Lane: Did you ever consider that you don't have friends because you don't share enough of yourself? Believe me, I know that isn't easy when you suffer from social phobia, but have you ever even considered that possibility? I'd love to get to know the real you—but you have to let me in.

Janet: I'm older than the rest of you and when I grew up, young women were supposed to be nice above everything else. I was taught that no one would like you if you were bossy or at all confrontational. And it went without saying that the woman was the peacemaker and nurturer in a relationship. Heaven forbid a woman would ever get angry! This is all so ingrained in me; it's part of me—it is who I am. I can't imagine changing my basic personality.

Richard: I'd suggest, Janet, that this is not who you are, but as you said, it is something you were taught was acceptable and desirable for a woman when you were growing up. But by being in this group you're saying it's not working for you.

Janet: No, it certainly isn't. I guess if I learned this, I might be able to unlearn it, but I can't imagine how I'd ever be able to do that.

This scenario exemplifies the middle stage of group in several ways. First, there is a high degree of self-disclosure. Second, group members are actively working toward their goals. Third, conflict arises in the group as Janet's interactional patterns are challenged by other group members, and Janet ultimately seems willing to start the painful process of change. Finally, mutual support and group cohesion is strong as seen in the group members' interactions first with Lori and later with Janet.

ENDING STAGE

The ending stage of groups focuses on feelings about termination and separation, on evaluation of the gains made in groups, and on ways members can continue their growth as they generalize their learning in group to everyday challenges (Corey et al., 1992). Group leaders must further ensure there are linkages to continued needed supports (Rooney & Chovanec, 2004).

The leader must plan for termination, preparing group members for it several weeks in advance. Termination needs to be discussed each session in open-ended groups due to the fluidity of membership. If a member is leaving, this needs to be announced in advance so that he/she and the other group members will have time to process and express their feelings about it (Corey et al., 1992).

In closed-ended groups with a fixed number of sessions, address termination several weeks before the final session. The group might prepare members by telling them about some typical reactions at this time, such as conflict, ambivalence, and negative feelings, and they can be encouraged to share these feelings (Corey et al., 1992; Toseland & Rivas, 2009). Other tasks include:

- Dealing with feelings of loss in other areas of members' lives in their past or current situations
- Discussing what members want to achieve during the remaining time
- Planning for the future
- Making referrals
- Evaluating the work of the group

- Establishing post group support systems
- Maintaining and generalizing change efforts

Termination is geared toward helping clients identify strategies so that change will be maintained and the momentum developed in group will continue to promote the desired change. While the practitioner does not want to imply that relapse is inevitable, the client must be prepared with strategies to enact if temptation presents itself or if the client begins to slip into old behaviors. Therefore, it is during termination that possibility rather than definitive phrasing is used. For example, "What *would* be the first thing you'd notice *if* you started to find things slipping back?" "What *could* you do to prevent things from going any further?" "*If* you have the urge to drink again, what *could* you do to make sure you didn't use?" might be typical inquiries to elicit strategies to use to protect against a return to old behavior.

Termination also involves maintaining change ("After you leave here, what will you be doing to keep things going in the direction you want?") and building on the changes that have occurred ("In the future, what will indicate to you that these changes are continuing to happen?") (Bertolino & O'Hanlon, 2002, p. 224). Questions are phrased to set up the expectation that change will continue to happen.

As well as group members commenting on their progress, termination should allow time to complete the standardized assessment instrument that was completed during the first session. This is obviously more easily done in a time-limited, closed-ended group. For open-ended groups, personnel are responsible for tracking when people enter and exit groups. The completion of assessment instruments would obviously have to happen in these cases before the first session (during intake or taking time before entering the first session) and immediately following the last session. Basic information on how long people attended group and for how many sessions would also have to be gathered.

Ceremonies often mark the endings of groups. Ceremonies may involve a party or potluck or giving out certificates of completion (Toseland & Rivas, 2009).

Question 7.1: Have you been involved in a group (or even a class) in which some kind of ceremony signified the last session?

UNPLANNED TERMINATION

Member Termination

Question 7.2: Consider a group that you have been involved with in the past (either as a member, a leader, or an observer). Did any unplanned terminations (group members quitting the group before the planned ending date) take place? What were the reasons (if known) for this? Write your answer here before reading on.

Yalom (1995) lists factors that may cause group members to drop out of treatment prematurely. Yalom points out that some members leave because of faulty selection processes and others are the result of flawed therapeutic technique. The main reasons are:

1. External factors, such as scheduling conflicts and changes in geographical location
2. Group deviancy (being the only "one" of anything)
3. Problems in developing intimate relationships
4. Inability to share the worker's time
5. Inadequate orientation to therapy
6. Complications arising from subgrouping (Toseland & Rivas, 2009, p. 382)

Leader Termination

Often interns leave at the end of their placements, but other common reasons for worker termination include a new job, a change in job responsibilities, illness, or pregnancy leave (Toseland & Rivas, 2009). To reduce disruption (Toseland & Rivas, 2009):

1. Tell group members as early as possible when termination will occur and share the reason for termination
2. Encourage members to freely discuss their feelings
3. Introduce the new leader to the group and, if possible, co-lead the group for awhile with the terminating worker

The following scenario involves a group held at a residential substance abuse treatment facility for adolescents. After reading the excerpt, decide what the group facilitator did well. If you were the leader, how would you approach this situation?

SW: I have an announcement to make. I have accepted a position at another organization. My last day at [residential substance abuse treatment facility for adolescents] will be in about three weeks. It was a difficult decision to come to, because I have enjoyed working with all of you, but it is a move that I need to make for my career. Looking around, it seems like some of you are having feelings about this. We've got some time now that we can use to begin to process this.

Client 1: I knew this was going to happen. I knew as soon as you said you had an announcement that it was going to be bad. First Mary left, then Heidi left, then Deborah left. I knew you'd be leaving too.

(Client 2 starts crying)

Client 3 *(angry)*: How could you do this? You're the one who kept telling me that I need to work on trusting people. You're the one that I decided to trust. How can you leave?

SW: My decision to leave has nothing to do with you. I've liked working with all of you, but by moving to a different agency, I'll be able to work with people that have a different set of challenges than you guys do. This move is the best thing for my career right now, and it's what I need to do, even though I will miss working with you all.

Client 2: Is there anything we can do so you'll change your mind? We'll be good, so you won't have to go.

SW: Like I said before, Client 2, I'm not leaving because of anything you guys have or haven't done. I've been working here for almost three years, and it's just time for me to move on.

Client 1: I'm going to have three different primary counselors in two months. Why should I even tell any of you anything? As soon as I share one of my secrets to staff, they leave.

SW: For those of you on my caseload, I know it will be difficult for awhile as you adjust to a new primary. Remember, though, that you're the one doing the work. Your new primary will help point you in the direction, but you're the one who has to decide if you're willing to work for your recovery, whether I'm here or not.

Client 3 *(yelling)*: What the hell is going on around here? Why are so many people leaving? Two primaries and both the family counselors in two months. What the hell is going on here that you're not telling us?

Client 2: Is this place going to close? What's going to happen to us?

Client 1: Yeah, are we closing down? Or are other staff leaving? I don't want to go sharing my secrets to just anyone if they're going to up and leave as soon as I've decided to go.

SW: There are no plans for this facility to close. Everyone is committed to you guys getting the best treatment possible. Sometimes organizations just go through periods of change where there is a lot of turnover in the staff. [Residential treatment program] is just doing that right now. And as far as I know, no one else has announced to the staff that they are planning on leaving. The county will make sure that there are always people here to provide you with the best treatment possible. Now we still have about three weeks before I leave. I'm going to be open to all of you during that time if you want to take a few minutes and talk and start to move towards closure.

Question 7.3: After reading the above excerpt, what did the group facilitator do well? If you were the leader, how would you approach this situation?

ALTERNATIVE CONCEPTUALIZATION OF GROUP DEVELOPMENT FOR MANDATED GROUPS

Because many of the groups social workers lead comprise non-voluntary clients, Rooney and Chovanec (2004) conceptualize the stages of groups as following the Transtheoretical Stages of Change model (Connors, Donovan, & DiClemente, 2001; Prochaska & Norcross, 1994) in which particular techniques and strategies are used to match the client's readiness to change. The primary focus is on building motivation for individuals to take action toward their goals and to maintain changes. As adapted to groups, precontemplation belongs to the beginning stage, whereas contemplation and action comprise the middle stage of the group's development. Termination (endings) involves maintenance of change and addressing relapse (Rooney & Chovanec, 2004).

These stages are summarized below.

Beginning Stage

The beginning stage of group is characterized by the *precontemplation* stage of change. In precontemplation, the individual believes there is no problem behavior and, therefore, is unwilling to do anything about it. At this stage, the individual sees the problem behavior as possessing more advantages than disadvantages. Typically, individuals in this stage are defensive and resistant about their behavior (Conners et al., 2001).

In the precontemplation stage, the group leader, rather than focusing on behavioral change, works on building client motivation to change and to increase awareness of the negative aspects of the problem behavior. (See Chapter 9.)

Middle Stage

In the middle stage of group, people are typically contemplating change. In the contemplation stage of change, individuals begin to believe there might be a problem, and they consider the feasibility and the costs of changing the behavior. The group leader helps the group members to enhance the advantages of changing (e.g., lessened legal consequences, improved health and relationships) and to work on ameliorating the disadvantages of changing. For example, if people use drugs to relate to others, the leader may focus on social skills training. The social support provided by the group can be used as a mechanism for change.

The middle stage of group also encompasses the *action* stage of change. In the action stage, the individual has started to modify the problem behavior and/or the environment in an effort to promote change in the past six months. The individual at this point is willing to follow suggested strategies and activities for change (Conners et al., 2001). In this stage, the group leader supports a realistic view of change by helping the individual achieve small, successive steps and acknowledging the difficulties associated with the early stages of change. Appraisal of high-risk situations and coping strategies to overcome these are a mainstay of this stage. Alternative reinforcers to problem behaviors can also be applied. The social support function of the group is drawn upon heavily so that change is promoted.

Ending Stage

It is important that group members are clear on the criteria needed for successful group completion (Rooney & Chovanec, 2004). The work during the *maintenance* stage of change is to plan for how to sustain and build upon changes that have been made. Attention is focused on avoiding slips or relapses (Prochaska & Norcross, 1994).

SUMMARY

This chapter has covered the stages of group development from a traditional standpoint and from the perspective of non-voluntary groups. Common trends of each stage have been discussed, although the stages are not necessarily clearly demarcated from each other. Therefore, the reader can note the general patterns that may arise in groups in which members have participated together for awhile. We will turn in the next couple of chapters to the beginning stage of group, a stage that all groups will have in common.

Chapter 8
Beginning the Group

In the beginning stage of group, members are often unsure of what is expected of them. They have uncertainties about whether they belong in the group and whether they may be helped in this way. They also feel nervous about revealing personal information and being vulnerable to others whom they do not know. These typical anxieties add to members' specific problems that brought them to group (Corey et al., 1992). To help people feel more comfortable with each other, some groups begin with introductions and icebreakers. Other beginning stage tasks covered in this chapter will be how to set up the first session for evaluation of group. Another beginning stage task is to cover group rules; this material has been extensively studied in Chapter 4.

INTRODUCTIONS AND OPENERS

After explaining the purpose of the group, the group members can start to get to know each other with introductions. At a minimum, this can entail each member stating his or her name. Icebreakers are useful both for learning names, for beginning some safe self-disclosure, and for easing the tension and anxiety of starting groups. Boxes 8.1 and 8.2 demonstrate some possible icebreakers, although there are many more, and you can feel free to create your own. Many of the icebreakers discussed in Box 8.1 have been used with teenagers, although they may also work with adults. Note that in non-voluntary groups for adults, it may feel "silly," "irrelevant," or "childish" to the members to start with icebreakers.

At the same time, Box 8.2's icebreakers focus on developing people's awareness of their strengths and resources and maybe helpful exercises in open-ended groups.

Box 8.1: Icebreakers

- A bag of candy is passed around the group. Each person is invited to take as much as he/she wants. For each piece of candy, the person has to share some personal information.

- In a variation of #1, a roll of toilet paper is presented to the group and each person is asked in turn to take "as much as he/she needs." For each square of toilet paper taken, the person has to reveal one piece of personal information.

- Have each person select a favorite song and describe how the lyrics describe that person's experience.

- Have group members throw a soft ball to each other; each person has to say the name of the persons preceding them and his or her own name before throwing the ball to the next person.

- Group members select an object from his or her wallet, purse, backpack, pocket, etc. that describes a quality about him or herself. Each member introduces him or herself and presents the object.

Box 8.2. Strengths-Based Icebreakers

1. Group members break into dyads, interview each other on some prepared questions, and then introduce the partner that has been interviewed to the group.

2. Members are asked about hobbies and interests: What do you do for fun?

3. What hobbies or interests do you have or have you had in the past? What skills and qualities have drawn you to these hobbies? What skills and qualities have you developed as a result? What kinds of activities are you drawn to?

4. Each person writes down one success and one challenge he or she has recently experienced in relation to the problem that has brought him or her to group.

5. Members "introduce themselves as the people they'd like to be at the time of their final session" (Corey et al., 1992, p. 61).

6. Each person is asked to talk about a quality of which he or she is proud.

7. Each person is invited to reflect on a personal quality or resource that has developed as a result of dealing with the problem that has brought them to group treatment. Without diminishing their suffering, people can be told that when they are able to find benefits from a stressor, they generally experience less depression and more well-being (Helgeson, Reynolds, & Tomich, 2006).

8. In groups in which people already know each other first, as in residential treatment, inpatient, and school settings, people write their names on a sheet of paper and identify two strengths. Papers are circulated to others in the group and then the members add other strengths they have noticed about each person until papers are returned to their original owner. As a final step, each person reads the list of strengths and comments aloud (Yalom 1985).

Question 8.1: What icebreakers have you been a part of as a group participant (say in a classroom or training)? Which ones did you especially like?

GOAL SETTING FOR GROUP WORK

The general purpose of the group can be individualized to each group member, so that members are motivated to make specific changes in their lives. Additionally, in formulating goals and announcing-them in front of the group, the members make a commitment in the presence of other people that they want to make some changes in their lives. This commitment process can be potentially powerful, and the group leader can emphasize that the group members are there to help each other with the commitments they have made.

Sometimes when people are mired in their symptoms, they have difficulty seeing beyond their cur rent unhappy circumstances, so the facilitator will need to assist the members in building a non-problem future before they may be able to consider the goals they seek. Conjuring a future when they are free from their current problems may fuel members' sense of hope, and, as we have noted, hope is a therapeutic factor in itself.

This process may also help individuals develop a blueprint for what changes need to be made. Future-oriented questions include the following:

- "What will be different about your life when group is successful?"

- "Imagine yourself in the future when the problem is no longer a problem. Tell me where you are, what you are doing and saying, and what others around you are doing and saying."

- "When this problem you have with anger [other problem behavior] disappears one day, how will you handle similar situations? What exactly will you do?"

When asking these questions, encourage people to talk about what they want to have different (the presence of positives) rather than what they don't want (the absence of negatives). The latter tendency keeps the focus on negative behavior rather than what is desired, whereas the former points firmly in the direction of change. For example, if, in a parenting group, a mother says, "I don't want to be yelling at my kids anymore," the group leader can ask, "What will you be doing instead of yelling?" Prepare to be persistent with this line of questioning since clients will often continue to talk about negative behaviors they wish to overcome rather than the positive behaviors needed to replace them.

Many times people are much more motivated for other people (their partners, their children) to change than they are to change themselves. In these instances, the group leader can talk about how we influence the behavior of other people by changing our own actions. The idea of a "dance" is often a helpful analogy for people to understand. If one is dancing with a partner and changes one's steps, the partner has no choice but to follow along in a different way.

An alternative way to tackle this type of client orientation is to ask, "What would you like (your child, partner) to be doing differently?" This question might have to be repeated or rephrased in order for people to come up with the presence of positive behaviors and ones that are behaviorally specific. In a domestic violence intervention group, one man argued that he shouldn't be in counseling; it was his wife who belonged there. Several other group members agreed. When the leader posed the above question, the man said, "If she'd stop complaining for once, it would help."

Group Leader:	What would you like her to do rather than complain?
Group member:	That's what she does—bitch, bitch, bitch—about money, and how she wants me to give her more money.
Group Leader:	What would you like to see her doing instead?
Group member:	Instead? That's a good question. It's hard to imagine.
Group Leader:	Spend a little time with that. The rest of you can think about this, as well. *(to the original group member)* Let's say I was videotaping the interaction between you, what would I see her doing?
Group member:	*(still obviously struggling with the concept)* I guess—I'd see her say "hi" when I came home and smile, maybe give me a kiss, rather than ask me if I got paid.

Group Leader:	What else?
Group member:	She'd ask me about my day rather than start complaining about the kids and what they need.
Group Leader:	So she would say hi when you came home, smile, give you a kiss, and ask you about your day.
Group Member:	Yeah, that would help. But that's never going to happen.
Group Leader:	And when she'd be doing those things you want, what would you be doing?
Group Member:	Well, I wouldn't be mad at her.
Group Leader:	What would you be doing instead?
Group Member:	I'd talk to her, tell her stuff that happened that day. She says I never talk to her, but I would if she stopped complaining for one minute.
Group Leader:	So you'd be talking to her about your day. What about when you came in the door?
Group Member:	I'd say "hi," too, kiss her.
Group Leader:	*(lets him absorb the image he has created for himself)* So what we will be doing in here is helping you create that kind of atmosphere in your home, that kind of communication that will get you what you want from your wife rather than the stuff you don't want.

You can see in this example that the group leader maintained a focus on the specific behaviors the group member would like to see from his wife rather than attending to the negative talk about her. The question "What will you be doing when she's doing those things?" presupposes the circular nature of people's interaction patterns. It implies the group member's role in the pattern he and his wife have created and has oriented him toward what he can work on in the group.

One specific type of group in which people think others should change is parenting groups. When I work with parents who believe their child, not them, should be involved in change efforts, I emphasize to them their importance to the child. "You are much more important to your children than I could ever be in our one hour a week, but they will change if you do react to them differently and take charge in different ways. You're the one with the most influence over them, not me." What parent would disagree with this statement?

Interestingly, a recent meta-analysis of parent training programs showed that programs in which parents only had training (rather than their children also receiving treatment) were more successful than when both parents and children were in treatment (Lundahl, Risser, & Lovejoy, 2006). The authors hypothesized that when parents only participated in parenting, they accepted responsibility for the changes that were made in their family instead of expecting their children to make changes. The results of this research can be shared with parents to help them buy into treatment.

SCALING INTERVENTIONS

We will detail here a solution-focused intervention called scaling questions, which encapsulate a number of techniques and are a powerful tool for goal-setting. Scaling questions involve the following steps and the process of scaling questions will be illustrated using a group held with teens involved in the juvenile justice system:

- Constructing the scale
- Choosing a goal
- Anchoring the goal
- Rank ordering and exception-finding
- Relationship questions
- Task-setting
- Measurement

Constructing the Scale: Have members construct a one-to-ten scale on a dry erase board, a chalkboard, or a piece of flip-chart paper (a surface visible enough for the other group members to see).

Choosing a Goal: Members are asked to select a goal they want to achieve from being a part of the group. For instance, boys in the juvenile offender group would usually select a goal, such as "staying out of trouble," and "following the terms of probation."

Anchoring the Goal: Anchor "10," as "when the goal will be achieved" or "when the problem is no longer a problem," "or when you know coming to group has been successful." A focus on "10" allows clients, who previously viewed their problems as "hopeless" and "overwhelming," to see the possibility of change, which gives them hope for the future.

My general guideline is to ask clients to describe in concrete and specific terms three behaviors and thoughts they will be having when they have reached "10." The reason behaviors and thoughts are a focus is that they are seen as more under clients' control than are feelings. Indeed, it can be explained to group members that it is easier to change their behaviors and thoughts than their feelings and that sometimes their feelings will shift after taking the necessary actions or changing their thoughts. For the most part, you want clients to identify the presence of positive behavior (e.g., "hanging around with straight friends") rather than the absence of negative behaviors (e.g., "staying away from gang-banging friends."). Other behaviors boys in the juvenile justice group would anchor at "10" included "going to school regularly," and "staying in after curfew." Thoughts they would be having included "It's not worth getting in trouble." Statements they would make are "I'm on probation, man, can't do it" (when others are trying to instigate criminal behavior in the client).

Rank Ordering and Exception-Finding: Group members rank themselves in relation to "10." Clients will often place themselves at a number implying change has already occurred, which allows them to see that their problems are not as all-encompassing as previously believed. The group leader can then inquire about the resources members have employed to get to where they are with questions such as "So you're already a four? What have you been doing to get yourself there?" Occasionally, clients place themselves at a "1"; in these cases, the group leader can ask what the person is doing to prevent problems from getting even worse.

Boys in the juvenile justice group would typically give themselves a lot of credit, ranking themselves at a six or so. They would state they felt these ratings were deserved as they were following through with the terms of probation, enacting some of the strategies they mentioned in their anchoring of "10." One note is that, as the group leader, you do not challenge group members on their ratings. For instance, you would not say, "A seven? You are not!" The way to get at discrepancy is to ask relationship questions, which are covered next.

Relationship Questions: involve asking people to rate themselves on their scale from the viewpoint of a person that is invested in their change (e.g., a partner, a parent, or a teacher). Very often clients view themselves differently from how others experience them. Inviting clients to perceive themselves from someone else's perspective may help them see themselves more realistically.

For instance, boys in the juvenile justice group were asked how their probation officers and their mothers would rate them. Generally, they would admit to lower ratings when viewed from these alternative perspectives. When I would ask about the difference in ratings, the boys would readily explain that their probation officers (who they generally placed about one rating behind their own) did not know how much they had changed, since the boys had usually not been in legal trouble for all their criminal behaviors. They explained their mothers' ratings as being lower still because of arguments at home around chores and following directions. The ratings of the boys' mothers let me know that more work needed to be done in group on communication with family members.

Task-Setting: in which group members are called upon to determine how they will move up one rank order by the time the next group meets. In the juvenile justice group, members would identify as their tasks that they would speak more respectfully to their parents and do more chores around the house.

Measurement of progress: Each week, a group check-in can center around where people are on their scale and on their completion of tasks. Progress continues to be monitored, which makes attainment toward goals quantifiable and measurable.

As one can see from these steps, the use of scaling interventions encapsulates many strengths-based techniques. After each step, group members can share their responses. This will help the group leader see if members understand what is being expected of them and sharing ideas helps others learn about what they can try differently. Further, the group leader can emphasize what will be covered in group to help people achieve what they have set out to do. Finally, the strengths focus of this intervention conducted in a group context can generate a sense of hopefulness and empowerment among members.

EVALUATION

Another part of beginning groups is to take time aside, ideally before any kind of intervention has taken place, for some type of formal evaluation. Students often believe the groups they run are successful based on their impressions and from feedback from the group members. However, one can gain a more objective sense of the group's progress by having the members complete standardized measurement tools. Therefore, attend in the planning stage to how you will evaluate groups.

Question 8.2: What do you see as other advantages of measuring progress of group members using a standardized measurement tool? Write your answer here before reading on.

There are several advantages of having group members complete measurement tools (Toseland & Rivas, 2009).

- Proof of progress can motivate group members to make further change
- To demonstrate the helpfulness of a group intervention to an agency or funding source
- Group leaders can assess client progress and see whether the group is meetings its purpose

Presented here is a general procedure to guide the group leader's efforts in using evaluation tools (Early & Newsome, 2004).

1. **Select a measure**: Selection of particular measures is determined by the purpose of the group (e.g., if the purpose is to reduce depression in group members, then use a measure on depression). This author has written other resource books on measures to use for certain populations and problems. Corcoran (2000) centers specifically on child and family problems; Corcoran and Walsh (2006) detail measures that involve DSM diagnoses, and Early and Newsome (2004) discuss measures that emphasize strengths for families. An additional assessment tool is the solution-focused scale (discussed earlier in this chapter). Tracked over time, the solution-focused scale can monitor member progress on a session-by-session basis.

2. **Time, space, materials**: Consider when the measure will be completed—at the beginning of the first session, during the orientation to the group, or during the intake for the program. Make available a hard writing surface—a desk or a clipboard—and appropriate writing utensils.

3. **Give the rational for the measure and explain how to fill it out**: Explain why group members are being asked to complete the scale. Familiarize yourself with the instrument beforehand so the explanation is clear and straightforward. In the explanation, assure clients there are no right or wrong answers.

4. **Answer questions, clarify**: Assess group members' literacy levels, and, if necessary, read each question and choice of responses to the group. If individuals are unsure of an answer, they should be encouraged to provide what they think is the "best" answer instead of the so-

cial worker interpreting the items or questions.

5. <u>Score the measure</u>: If the measure is easy to score, the group leader can provide instructions, and the members can score their own measures for immediate feedback. If the scoring protocol is more difficult, the group leader may instead choose particular items for discussion, such as "What did you learn about yourself from filling out the scale?" or "Does it give you more ideas on what to work on?" If there are strengths-based items, some elaboration might be given by group members on how they were able to create exceptions to "the problem" (see Chapter 11). If there are deficit-based items (which are typical), members can still center on "sometimes" responses to items, which indicates that other times there is not a problem. They can be asked about these times, "What's different? What are you doing differently?"

6. <u>File the measure</u>: The completed measure should be filed and treated as confidential information. Have completed measures available for later follow-up and assessment of outcomes.

7. <u>Repeat the measure at a later date</u>: Administer the same measure one or more times subsequent to the first time (the end of the last group session and possibly a follow-up). Use identical procedures each time the measure is repeated.

SUMMARY

This chapter has covered some of the tasks involved in the beginning of groups: providing introductions and icebreakers; goal-setting; and evaluation. As mentioned earlier in the text, social workers may lead groups in which membership revolves each session. In these types of groups, valuable group time cannot be spent on icebreakers and evaluation of incoming members each time. Therefore, the content of this chapter has to be adapted to the needs of the particular group. As also emphasized previously, social workers will often lead groups with people who have been mandated to attend. Ways to approach these groups will be covered in the next chapter.

Chapter 9
Techniques for Working with Mandated Groups

Social workers often facilitate groups that serve people who are mandated to treatment by the legal system. Such people face possible negative consequences if they decide not to attend, such as not getting their children returned to them, incarceration, probation, or suspension of their driving privileges. When I was a student intern in my concentration placement, I co-led an open-ended group with my supervisor for parents who had physically abused or neglected their children (or their partners had done so). She would shout at members and confront them with their behaviors as I sat mostly quiet, feeling very uncomfortable. When we processed the group afterward, she coached me to use her approach, but I just couldn't do it. At the time, I thought, I'm never going be able to lead groups if it means shouting at people. Fortunately, over the years I've learned about other approaches that indicate more respect for the individual, one of the central tenants of social work, and that I believe are more effective.

The following techniques are ways to address groups with mandated clients when they are at the beginning stages of change (see Chapter 7). These techniques are not all used with every group; rather implement them selectively when the needs of the population arise.

- Prepare an opening statement/script
- Clarify role expectations
- Align with the client's position and perspective
- Use relationship questions
- "Side with" the resistance

The following scenario is a closed-ended group for mothers in the child welfare system who have had their children taken away and placed into foster care. This is the second session of a 10-week group.

Marge (group leader):	I thought we could start by asking if anyone would like to share how they are feeling today and why. (Pause) Alice, would you like to start?
Alice:	I don't know how I'm feeling; I just know that this just isn't how it's supposed to be. I am a very good mother. I make sure my kids are fed and have shoes on their feet. I have a full-time job and haven't done any drugs for a long time. Just because a friend asked me to hold onto his pot for him, now I'm the one being punished. I had let my friend off in a downpour and he thought his pot might get wet. I just couldn't say, "No." I told them I'd take a piss test, but they didn't even listen. Now my kids are in some foster home with six other kids. They say I have to stay clean to get my kids back, but I'm already clean.

(Alice starts crying and the woman next to her is getting her some tissue.)

Susan: I'll go next, because I am pissed off! That's how I'm feeling! They took my daughter just because I walked two doors over to borrow something from a neighbor. She is only two-years-old and she was napping—how much trouble can she get in? This isn't right! My daughter was taken from me by the court-appointed Guardian ad Litem. They treat me like I have no rights. What does some court-appointed stranger know about taking care of my kid? That guardian didn't even look like she was old enough to be a mother! This is a screwed up system we have in this country.

Tracey: I know exactly what you mean. They gave custody of my kids to my ex-husband. He's the REAL drinker. But he cleaned himself up real nice for court and they believed everything he said, and now I don't have my kids. *(She goes on at great length about how she only drinks a little each day but her ex-husband gets really drunk when he drinks.)* They need to change the system!

Marge: *(after a pause)* I wonder if anyone else would like to share.

Question 9.1: What do you see going on in the group? Is this appropriate for the type of group, its purpose, and its duration?

PREPARE AN OPENING STATEMENT

In your introduction to the group after you explain its purpose, you can acknowledge that people feel they have been coerced into treatment. But also bring to their attention that they did have options—attend the treatment or accept the legal consequences—and congratulate them for having made a good choice (Rooney & Chovanec, 2004). You can state your understanding that they might feel angry and resentful about the reasons they were referred to treatment, but that the group time is too valuable to spend talking about the unfairness of it at all. You can end by saying that everyone can get something out of the group, even if they don't believe they belong initially. In a court-mandated anger management group, the group leaders talk about how teaching the curriculum has been beneficial for them personally in managing some of life's difficulties. This helps to destigmatize the reason members are in group; it is not because they are "crazy" or "disturbed," but that people from all walks of life can benefit from the training.

Question 9.2: Using the above scenario, write an opening statement based on how you would begin this group .

CLARIFY ROLE EXPECTATIONS

Members might not be clear about why they are in group treatment, the advantages of treatment, and the consequences if they do not attend and/or participate (Toseland & Rivas, 2009). For example, in the group I led with juvenile offenders who typically only attended once with group membership changing each session, a group member occasionally acted disruptively, and ignoring the behavior or simple redirection did not help. At that point, I would ask, "What's your understanding of this group?" Group members at that point would typically be unable to answer, and I would redirect the question to the other participants. In every case, clarifying expectations about the group acted to get the disruptive behavior "in line."

Question 9.3: Using the above scenario, how would you get the group members to be clear about the expectations of the group?

ALIGN WITH THE CLIENT'S POSITION AND PERSPECTIVE

People who are mandated to treatment often would like to argue about the fact that they do not belong in the group. Rather than getting into this argument, the group leader can convey acceptance of the client's perspective. If the practitioner becomes polarized from a client's position, the client is likely to become defensive and even more entrenched in a position against change (Berg, 1994) as you will see in the following scenario.

In this case, a social work intern was allowed to observe a substance abuse treatment group for both outpatient and inpatient clients at a psychiatric hospital. A new client, James, entered the group.

James:	I don't even know why I'm here. I have no plans of stopping my drinking any time soon.
Dave:	Well, you wouldn't have even thought of coming, much less come, if you didn't have plans of ever quitting.
Matt:	I agree.
Sam:	Me, too. I was where you were—denial.
James:	I'm not in denial. I'm just honest. I'm not like you guys. I have no desire to quit. My dad died a drunk, and he was a good man. So if it was good enough for him, then it's good enough for me.
Matt:	Then why are you here?
James:	I don't know. This is a waste of time.
Facilitator:	What do you mean a waste of time?

James:	Have you not been listening? I don't plan on quitting. I don't want to talk about quitting, so this group is then a waste of time. I'm gonna leave and go home.
Matt:	Come back when you're ready to talk.
Facilitator:	Why don't you stay until the end and listen to the others? We also are giving job training information.
James:	I don't want to listen to anyone else complain. I can go to my sister's house for that.
Facilitator:	No, why don't you go ahead and stay? I think you would really get use out of the job training info.
James:	You think? You don't know me. And if I recall, this is an open-ended group, and that means I can come and leave when I want.

(This exchange went back and forth for about five more minutes until James got up and left the group.)

James obviously felt defensive and "put on the spot" by the member confrontations as soon as he entered the group. He went as far as to say he had no plans of quitting at all. Obviously, there is more ambivalence present–he is in a treatment facility whether mandated or not. This scenario shows how people might "dig in their heels" if they are feeling defensive and not allow the other part of their ambivalence to emerge.

One technique in such a situation is for the group leader to position him or herself so that he or she is aligned with the client against external entities that are desirous of the client's change. The way to do this is through questioning as follows: "James, whose idea was it that you come to group?" [After James answers,] "I wonder what we need to do here to convince... [the judge, your caseworker, your probation officer] that you don't need to come here anymore?" By orienting group members toward the requirements of their mandates, you can involve clients in goal-setting rather than in convincing them of their need to attend group.

USE RELATIONSHIP QUESTIONS

When clients resist being in a group, relationship questions—those that ask members to view themselves from the perspective of another person—are helpful in moving the client past the resistance (De Jong et al., 2008). When people are stuck in a problem, they find it difficult to see alternatives. By viewing the problem from another person's point of view ("What would your wife/boss/mother say needs to happen in this group to know that our time has been successful?"), they can sometimes see other possibilities. Relationship questions have the added advantage of allowing people to increase their ability to take on other people's perspectives and see the impact of their behavior on other people.

Question 9.4: How could you use a relationship question in the scenario of "James" above?

Question 9.5: Referring to the closed-ended group scenario for mothers in the child welfare system at the beginning of the chapter, how might you use relationship questions?

"SIDE WITH" THE RESISTANCE

Sometimes clients who have been entrenched in a negative position vis-à-vis change will start to argue from the other side of their ambivalence when the group leader joins with their position. The leader completely agrees with—even exaggerates—the client's views if ambivalence is detected. When all resistance is removed, a paradoxical effect often occurs, causing group members to take the other side of the argument for change (Miller & Rollnick, 2002). For example, with James in the scenario above, the group leader might agree, "I can see your point. Why would you want to stay here when you have no intention of quitting?" James might then start to backpedal and say, "Well, I was thinking about it, but now I'm not so sure anymore." As a further example, in a group for domestic violence offenders, one member, after thoroughly describing his wife as a despicable person, was told by the group leader, "Wow, she sounds like a monster! I can't imagine how you ever managed to stay with her this long!" The surprised member immediately replied, "Well, she's not THAT bad."

One exercise at the beginning of mandated groups is for members to write down all the reasons they do not belong in group and then the group leader reads them aloud (without identifying who said what). This is also a good technique to use when you are referring people to Alcoholics Anonymous or other 12-step groups when they are reluctant to go—ask them to note how they do not fit into the group.

Question 9.6: What do you think the purpose of such an exercise is? Write your answer here before reading on.

The purpose of this exercise is to "side with people's resistance." Generally, when people are mandated to a group intervention, they are defensive and do not believe they have a problem. By "going with" this side of their ambivalence (because ambivalence is typically present with problem behaviors and the prospect of changing them), you activate the other part of the ambivalence (the part that wants to change).

Use Techniques to Approach Resistance from Motivational Interviewing

In motivational interviewing, the group leader reflects members' comments that deny or argue against the existence of a problem; however, the group leader uses language both directively and selectively to move the group member toward change (Moyers & Rollnick, 2002). This is shown when members blame others and fail to take responsibility for their actions. In these situations, the group leader reflects the clients' statements back, leaving out the parts that make them unaccountable for their actions (Bertolino & O'Hanlon, 2002). The following example involves an anger control group.

Another way to use language selectively is to emphasize the part of the client that wants to change.

Group member:	He called me a name, so I hit him.
Group leader:	You hit him.
Group member:	She yelled at me, so I yelled back.
Group leader:	You yelled at your aunt.

Recall the scenario of the substance abuse treatment group at the state psychiatric hospital. The student intern asked group members to talk about a time they had an urge to use but did not do so. See how the social work intern responded in the following excerpt so that the group member's statements are selectively affirmed.

John:	I remember one time. I had to go to work, and I didn't use.
Social Work Intern:	You said earlier that you used a lot and still went to work. What was different about this time?
John:	Well, I knew that if I got fired from this job it would be harder to get money to get drugs so I didn't want to lose my job.
Social Work Intern:	So, it sounds like you didn't want to lose your job.

We will cover specific techniques from motivational interviewing that include simple reflection, amplified reflection, double-sided reflection, shifting focus, agreement with a twist, clarifying free choice, and constructing a decisional balance.

- *Simple reflection* involves acknowledgment of a client's feeling, thought, or opinion so that the client continues to explore his or her problem rather than becoming defensive ("You're not sure you're ready to spend a lot of time changing right now") [Carroll, 1998]. Simple reflection allows further exploration rather than evoking defensiveness.

Question 9.7: Recall the scenario on page 105. How would you use "simple reflection" with James?

- *Amplified reflection* goes beyond simple reflection in that the group member's statement is acknowledged but in an extreme fashion. The purpose of such a statement is to bring out the side of the client that wants to change. An amplified reflection, such as the statement, "You really like drinking, and you don't think you'll ever want to change," typically has the effect of getting the client to back down from an entrenched position, allowing for the possibility of negotiation about change (Moyers & Rollnick, 2002).

Question 9.8: How would you use "amplified reflection" with James?

- *Double-sided reflection* reflects both aspects of the client's ambivalence. When people are exploring the possibility of change, they are divided between wanting to change and also wanting to keep the behavior that has become problematic ("You're not sure cocaine is that big a problem, and at the same time a lot of people who care about you think it is, and getting arrested for drug possession is causing some problems for you" [Carroll, 1998]). Double-sided reflection can also pull the client's attention to the inconsistency between the person's problem behavior and his or her goals and values (Moyers & Rollnick, 2002) ["Your relationship is very important to you, and your drug use is causing problems in the relationship].

Question 9.9: How would you use "double sided reflection" with James?

- *Shifting focus* involves moving the group member's attention from a potential impasse to avoid becoming polarized from the client's position. When the person begins to argue against what the facilitator might feel is the best course, the leader can immediately shift his or her position and redirect the focus ("I think you're jumping ahead here. We're not talking at this point about you quitting drinking for the rest of your life; let's talk some more about what the best goal is for you and how to go about making it happen"). The general guideline for shifting focus "is to first defuse the initial concern and then direct attention to a more readily workable issue" (Miller & Rollnick, 2002, p. 102).

Question 9.10: How would you use "shifting focus" with James?

- *Agreement with a twist* involves agreement with some of the group member's message but in a way that then orients the client in the direction towards change ("I can see why you'd be troubled about you and your wife's arguments about your use. I wonder what needs to happen so you don't need to keep talking about this").

- *Clarifying free choice* involves communicating that it is up to the client whether he or she wants to change, rather than getting embroiled in a debate or an argument about what the client must do ("You can decide to take this on now or wait until another time"). "When people perceive that their freedom of choice is being threatened, they tend to react by asserting their liberty. Probably the best antidote for this reaction is to assure the person of what is surely the truth: in the end, it is the client who determines what happens" (Miller & Rollnick, 2002, p. 106).

Question 9.11: How would you "clarify free choice" with John? (see page 108).

- A normal development in the beginning of group is for people to feel ambivalent about attending ("I don't know whether or not I belong here") and about change. This is obviously greatly exacerbated when people are mandated into treatment. One way to address the ambivalence about change with mandated clients is to bring it out into the open with a discussion about the advantages and disadvantages of the problem behavior. This process is called a *decisional balance* in motivational interviewing terms (Miller & Rollnick, 2002).

Discussing the advantages and disadvantages of the problem behavior can be seen as a strengths-based technique as it assumes people engage in negative behaviors because it serves them well in some ways (rather than seeing them as self-destructive). At the same time, we can assume that healthy options to meet these same needs do exist. Further, this technique, called the "decisional balance," assumes that people demonstrate "ambivalence," rather than resistance, to change (Miller & Rollnick, 2002). In the process of helping group members identify the advantages of changing, the group leader can affirm any change statements people make. Finally, pinpointing the advantages of the problem behavior indicates what the group members need. For example, if a number of people in a group for parents who have physically abused their children reveal that they enjoy the release of anger that comes with punishing their children, working on anger control techniques would be essential. If people recognize that they are unable to relate to others without using substances, they might be taught how to manage social situations.

- The tactic of initially inquiring about the *benefits of the problem behavior* disarms people because they are steeled to defend themselves against a treatment provider who is going to try to force them to change. By being allowed to discuss the benefits ("How is this working for you?" "What do you get out of this?"), members typically begin to feel more comfortable and understood. Some people have not previously spent time examining the reasons for the use of a bad habit and may gain insight from hearing other members reveal their motivations.

Having been allowed to talk about the benefits, spontaneous discussions of the disadvantages might ensue (e.g., "It sure is fun to stay out late partying with my friends, but the next day those hangovers are a killer.") If not, the group leader can inquire about "the not so good things" about the problem behavior. Note the phrasing which tends to keep people's defensiveness low. As people talk about the disadvantages of their problems, the group leader lists them in writing for the group as a whole just as he or she did for the advantages.

As an example of a decisional balance, I will present some possible responses that group members mandated to treatment for physically abusing their children might make. In this illustration, you will note how the group leader can respectfully counter some of the members' rationales for physical discipline which, in the past, has led to actual abuse. Of course, it is always better if group leaders can elicit from the group members some counterarguments before they do so as feedback coming from peers will be a more potent influence.

Advantages of Physical Discipline

1. **Children obey**

    Counterargument: From the standpoint of behavioral theory, physical discipline trains children to disobey until parents become physical with them. Therefore, children tend to escalate their acting out behavior until this point is reached.

2. **Release of anger is a relief**

   Counterargument: Group members can work on developing awareness of when anger builds, on how to circumvent escalation, and on taking time-outs for themselves.

3. **Children know who's in charge/respect parents**

   Counterargument: An important goal of authoritative parenting is to have and enforce clear and consistent rules and to monitor children's whereabouts and activities (Steinberg, 2001). However, the use of physical discipline is not necessary in attaining this goal.

4. **Parents want children to succeed in life and to be tough against adversity; they believe that physical discipline is a way to achieve these goals.**

   Counterargument: Authoritative parenting (see #3) can help children be successful. Additionally, as mentioned in point #1, children learn to act out until they are physically punished. This sets children up for a difficult time in school and most of the "outside world" where physical punishment is not used yet compliance with the rules is required. Also, children who are physically punished by their parents to gain compliance will more likely use physical force themselves with peers, which will hardly set them on a successful path in school, the workplace, and in peer relationships.

5. **Group members' parents may have physically abused them, so they believe it is an appropriate way to manage children's misbehavior.**

   Counterargument: Explore the subsequent result on the relationship between parent and child due to physical punishment. Ask parents how they would like things to be different for their children and for the parent-child relationship. Also discuss changes in societal attitudes about physical discipline.

Disadvantages of Abusive Behavior

For the parent:

- Guilt
- Possible legal consequences
- Authorities are involved in family life
- May cause intergenerational transmission of aggression

For the child:

- Children may feel negatively toward the person enacting the punishment and toward the source of the behaviors for which they are being punished (e.g., homework, other siblings).
- Teaches children aggression by modeling aggression.
- Teaches children what they shouldn't do, but not what they should do.
- Is correlated with an array of problems in youth (aggression, impulsivity, social skill deficits, language problems, low IQ, and internalizing problems (Kolko & Wenson, 2002).

Research findings indicate physical abuse is correlated for children with: 1) aggression/behavior problems; 2) poor impulse control; 3) social skills deficits; 4) cognitive deficits in terms of language and IQ/academic problems; 5) trauma-related symptoms, such as anxiety and depression (Kolko & Wenson, 2002).

As group members talk about the disadvantages of problem behavior, the group facilitator will selectively affirm change talk and ask members to elaborate on statements about change: "You would really like to wake up one morning with a clear head." Additionally, group leaders can listen for the goals and values that people have for themselves (e.g., health, future well-being, success, improved relationships) and highlight the discrepancy between these and the current problem behavior: "You want to keep this job so you'll be able to buy a car, and you have a hard time functioning at work—or even getting there at times—because of your hangovers."

The following excerpt returns again to the inpatient substance abuse treatment group session in which members were discussing times they were triggered to use but chose not to do so.

> **Sue:** Yeah, I can relate. I have two kids and one that CPS already took because of my using. I can remember one time I was on the street and I had my last bit of money and I was going to give it to the dope man, but something in me just stopped. I had a picture of my daughter in my mind, and I knew she needed food. So I went on home.
>
> **Social Work Intern:** So it sounds like for you, your children were big factors in stopping you from using on that occasion. How about the rest of you?

Question 9.12: At this point, what could the intern say that would further explore the discrepancy between the client's values and goals and her current substance use?

In the group I have described with teen boys, I presented members with a list of values, which they rank ordered in importance for themselves. Then each member created a picture, highlighting a priority value and depicting how he could experience it in a pro-social way. Some teens identified "freedom" as most important; they drew pictures and discussed strategies of how to avoid "getting locked up," which resulted in a loss of freedom. Spending time with girlfriends was recognized as a way not only to get more "love," but also as a way to stay away from negative peers. Teens mentioned playing sports and talking to girls as ways they could get "excitement" without committing illegal acts.

Question 9.13: Refer to the adult sex-offender group in which the group member was to present his sexual history to the group. Can you see an opportunity for a decisional balance within this scenario? If so, what behaviors might you focus upon?

SUMMARY

Social workers may often facilitate groups in which clients are mandated to attend. Because many mandated clients will tend to be members of socially diverse groups, the reader is urged to consult Chapter 15 for approaches to group work with multicultural populations. The focus of this chapter has been on techniques from both solution-focused therapy and motivational interviewing to help the leader engage group members who may be angry or resistant to change. Such techniques are designed to help group leaders avoid power struggles and instead build collaboration among the members and the group leader, which can enhance the process of change.

Chapter 10
Making the Most Out of Ending
and Beginning Subsequent Sessions

Although group sessions will be marked by varying formats, valuable therapeutic work may emerge at the end of sessions and at the beginning of subsequent sessions. This chapter will devote itself to this topic so that facilitators can learn how to use these segments of time in a purposeful fashion.

ENDING SESSIONS

The ending of sessions involves *closure* of the work, *evaluation* of group members' commitment to the group process and discussion of member's *progress* toward goals, and *plans* for the next session. Although time may occasionally slip away, you want to avoid ending group abruptly (e.g., "Okay, time's up!") and instead give time to these processes (Corey et al., 1992).

Closure

The first part of ending groups involves *closure*, which involves "eliciting a few words from each person about the highlights of the session" (Corey et al., 1992, p. 74) through the use of certain questions:

- "What did we do today that you felt made a difference?" (to learn what is instigating change and what is helpful in the process)
- "Could you briefly summarize what this session has meant to you?"
- "What was the most important thing you experienced during this meeting?"
- "Could you summarize the important thoughts or insights you're taking with you?"
- "What touched you most in other people's work today?"
- "Before we go, is there any feedback you want to give to someone else here?"
- "What did you learn about yourself?"

During closure, leaders may also summarize the meeting, share their reactions, and remark on the process of the group, such as group cohesion, people's willingness to risk talk about sensitive topics, and the ability of members to interact with each other (Corey et al., 1992).

Evaluation

The second part of ending groups involves *evaluation* in terms of what members are both giving and receiving from the group through the following types of questions (Corey et al., 1992, p. 152):

- "Did you get what you wanted from this session?"
- "Are you satisfied with your level of participation in this session?"
- "If you are apathetic, bored, uninvolved, hostile, or resistant, what are you willing to do (if anything) to change this attitude?"

Evaluation also includes *discussion of members' progress toward goals*. The group leader can ask people about the steps that need to be taken between the present session and the next to make changes toward their goals. One way, through homework, to focus people's awareness on their resources and the times they are empowered to appropriately deal with their problems is through a variation of a generic solution-focused task. In this task, the group leader states, "Between now and the next session, observe when the problem is not occurring or is just a little better, and pay attention to how you are able to make that happen" (Murphy, 1997).

Some groups require homework; a review of the homework assignment at the end of the session may then be necessary. In other groups, homework is optional and there can be a great deal of latitude and creativity in devising tasks. For instance, the leader may assign homework as the need arises, members can come up with their own tasks, or they can be suggested by other participants (Corey et al., 1992).

Planning

The final piece at the end of groups involves *planning*, looking ahead to the next meeting and asking for input with the following questions:

- "Are there ways in which you would like to be different in the next session?"
- "Was there anything unfinished for you today that you would like to continue in our next meeting?"

Sometimes a client's work will be cut off because group time has elapsed. Rather than setting a precedent of extending the length of the session, the leader can ask the member with the unfinished work to state what he or she would like to accomplish the next time the group meets (Corey et al., 1992). In the specific case of conflict between members, the leader may make a statement such as the following: "There is too much here to thoroughly address today, but we have made progress just by opening up communication around this. Since we are limited right now, we'll be sure to start here next session." This type of statement reassures members that the leader will not ignore or avoid conflict. At times, members may start conflict (or bring up other difficult topics) when they know there will be an easy "out," i.e., the end of a session. If this is a pattern for one or more members, the leader may note this tendency and bring this into the discussion.

BEGINNING SUBSEQUENT SESSIONS

We will talk about different ways to start sessions depending on the type of group. In many structured, time-limited treatment groups, for example, cognitive-behavioral groups, homework is often a requirement; therefore, sessions begin by an opening check-in on the homework assignment. Therefore, we will take some time to discuss this process.

Another way to start sessions is particularly germane to open-ended groups in which membership revolves frequently, as in in-patient psychiatric or substance-abuse treatment facilities. These sessions may involve members who have attended for only a few sessions and those who have just begun.

Homework

Another way to start a session is to go over the homework that was assigned from the previous session.

Question 10.1: What will happen if a group leader assigns homework and then doesn't check in with people about completing it? Write your answer here before reading on.

If a group leader does not follow up with homework assignments, he or she conveys the message that neither the homework nor the effort group members have made are important. It takes away the opportunity for people to have their accomplishments recognized by group members. Further, it might decrease people's motivation to work between sessions toward their goals. Finally, not checking in with homework makes the leader seem disorganized (Toseland & Rivas, 2009).

Question 10.2: What can you do in group if members, in a structured group that emphasizes homework completion, admit they did not complete the agreed-upon task? Write your answer here before reading on.

In general, the group leader should reinforce homework behavior rather than non-compliance. By saying "Oh, that's okay," or "No problem," clients will get the message that tasks are not important. In the case of non-completion of homework, the group leader can spend time inquiring about what got in the way and negotiating the task for the following week. It could be, for instance, that the task was too ambitious for the client, and it needs to be broken down into smaller, more manageable pieces. Webster-Stratton and Herbert (1993) have a series of recommended questions to ask when the client has difficulty following through with tasks:

What makes it hard for you to do the assignment?

- "How have you overcome this problem in the past?"
- "What advice would you give to someone else who has this problem?"
- "What can you do to make it easier for you to complete the assignment this week?"
- "What thoughts come to mind when you think about this assignment?"
- "What makes it hard to do?"
- "Does this seem relevant to your life?"
- "How could we make this more helpful?" or "What assignment might be more useful for you?"

If the task did not work out as planned, the group leader can convey there is no such thing as a failure. Instead the focus can be on, "What did you learn? What needs to be done differently next time?" This reinforces the usefulness of homework and encourages group members to continue applying what they gain in group through homework assignments.

BEGINNING GROUP SESSIONS

Question 10.3: Have you heard group leaders start with either of these openers: *"Why are you here?" "Let's start with how everyone is feeling today?" "Let's go around the room and check in."* What do you think of these opening lines? Are they effective or not? Write your answer here before reading on.

Yalom (1985) writes of several problems with such openers. First, the responses to this question are "several steps removed from the work one can do in a therapy group" (p. 212). Second, they emphasize the "then and there," so that they cannot make use of the main resource of the group, which is to deal with "here and now" interpersonal patterns and reactions. Third, most of a session may be consumed by the admission stories of new members. Specific to the question of feelings, it fails to orient members toward changing their feelings. Finally, the answers provide no blueprint for how group work can proceed.

Given these limitations, Yalom (2005) recommends that the group leader ask each member, in round-robin fashion, what he/she would like to get out of a session before focusing on a particular person (Corey, 2008; Yalom, 2005). He calls this process *agenda-setting* and advises that the focus, as much as possible, should be on interpersonal relations, can be worked on in the here-and-now of the group, and can be accomplished in a single session. If a group member brings up a problem that is too large for a single session (to get help for depression) or one that is anchored in the past ("I've lost my job and need to find a new one"), the following questions can be posed (Yalom, 2005):

- "Has the person's interpersonal style contributed to the current problem?"
- "Has the person's way of relating gotten in the way of obtaining help and solving the problem?"

Yalom (1985) lists several advantages to this approach. First, it gives the session structure. The group leader can formulate a rough agenda for group, and take into account people's related concerns. Second, people take an active role in their work. People are asked to be explicit about their needs, a particularly therapeutic exercise for those who habitually ask for help in indirect or self-destructive ways. Third, this go-round process allows people who are in crisis or who are at risk of dropping out of the group to have their concerns addressed. For example, in a group for Post-Traumatic Stress Disorder (PTSD) victims of combat, a member says, "I feel like I'm ready to snap and this group isn't helping at all, even though I've been coming here for three weeks now. I don't have a family. I leave work and go back to my empty apartment and watch TV till it's time to go back to work. At work they tell me I have a bad attitude. What do they expect from a guy who can't sleep? The sleeping pills make me sleep, but I still have nightmares and wake up feeling drugged." When asked what he would like to have happen in the group, he says, "I don't know. I guess that I'd feel better and be able to sleep; I just need to sleep." In this example, attention would need to focus on this man's concerns so that he feels that the group is addressing his needs. Although personal agendas may vary, Yalom (1985) states that most boil down to the ones outlined in Table 10.1.

For example, in a women's group at an inpatient psychiatric hospital, a woman who had been admitted for suicidality responded initially to the idea of an agenda that she just wanted to feel better, because she felt so terrible, but she didn't think anything could help. The group facilitator persisted in asking, "If something were to help, what would that be?" The woman paused, then admitted, a little sheepishly, that maybe if the group paid her some attention.... The group leader commended her for asking directly for attention rather than by threatening suicide and asked how much time she wanted to take of the group.

Table 10.1. Common Personal Agendas for Group Sessions

Agenda	Specific Questions
Loneliness	How have you felt lonely in here? From whom have you cut yourself off in this group and how have you done that?
Poor communication	With whom in this room is your communication good? With whom is it not entirely satisfactory? With whom here in this room would you like to improve your communication?
Expression of feelings	Would you be willing to express the feelings you have here in the group as they occur?
Assertion	Would you try to say one thing that you'd ordinarily suppress? Would you select the people in the group today that most overwhelm you, and see if you might be able to explore some of your feelings about that? Would you like to ask something for yourself? How much time would you like for yourself later in the group today?
Closeness with others and making friends	With whom here in this room would you like to get closer? Would you try some different way of approaching them today? Would you like feedback from them on how you create distance?
Trust	Would you try to explore that with members of this group? Who in this room do you particularly trust? Why? What is there about them? What do you have to fear from anyone here in this group? In which ways do I threaten you? What do you have to fear from me?
Feedback on how one comes across to others	Why do you want the feedback? [tie in with some important aspect of the person's problem with living.] What aspect of yourself would you like some feedback about? From whom here in the room do you especially want some feedback today?
Expressing anger	So as not to scare other group members, people are encouraged to talk about minor anger, such as irritation and annoyance toward others.

A second person in the group said she had turned to drugs because their effects were predictable. She experienced people, on the other hand, as unpredictable and dangerous. With the facilitator's assistance, she formulated an agenda of wanting to talk about with whom in the group she felt safest and with whom she did not feel as safe.

A third member talked about feeling conflicted in wanting to be left alone versus being with others; she felt afraid that if she let people in, they would try to take over and not respect her space. The agenda consisted of telling other group members with whom she felt it would be easiest to set boundaries around and with whom it would be most difficult. Additionally, she would talk about with whom she was most afraid of being controlled in the group.

A fourth spoke about feeling left out when she was with women. Her subsequent tactic was to isolate and pretend she didn't want to be included. As a result, she felt cut off and lonely. She wanted to ask how she came across to people because of her sense of "not fitting in." She also wanted to attempt to be part of the group and see how people received that.

One woman said she felt critical and judgmental of others, and found reasons not to become close with people; as a result she had few friends. She decided to talk to the group members about toward whom she has felt judgmental. She agreed to explore if there were parts of herself she saw in that person, or if there were qualities she admired.

A woman who was bulimic understood that some kind of interpersonal disappointment would typically set off her binges, usually when her feelings were hurt. Who seemed the least likely to hurt her? Who was she afraid were going to let her down? What did she think they might do?

In this particular group, people were validated to find out that others shared some of their fears about relationships and loneliness. Themes of safety and trust were common as was uncertainty about how one came across in an interpersonal context.

The following scenario involves the morning meeting in a locked inpatient psychiatric unit at a general hospital. The morning meeting lasts for thirty minutes and orients clients to the schedule of the day. All clients are asked to introduce themselves and they may choose to tell the group in a few sentences why they are in the hospital. If they want to talk at length they are encouraged to talk to the leader or their nurse after the group.

Leader : *(To group member A)* Would you like to introduce yourself?

A: Yes, I'm A, and I'm here for suicidal thoughts

Leader: Thank you, A. I'm glad you're here.

Leader: *(To group member B)* Could you introduce yourself to the group? It's up to you if you want to say why you are here

B: Okay, my name is B, and I'm here for medication management, and I'm voluntary.

Leader: Thank you, B. *(to C)* Would you like to share your name with the group?

C: Yes, I'm C.

Leader. Thank you, C. Do you want to share why you are here, C?

C: No, it's private.

Leader: Okay, I respect that. I'm glad you came today.

C: I'm (*&^%$) not glad I came here! The judge wants me to stay for five days. I have stuff to do.

Leader: Could you please not use bad language? Did you just find this out, C?

C: Uh huh.

Leader: I understand that you are upset. Is it possible for you to sit down?

C: No I ain't staying. *(C throws a cup of water against a wall)*

Leader: C, you are scaring the other patients. You need to leave group and talk to your nurse. I can talk with you after group if you are calmed down.

(Some of the patients leave the group. C stands there, then sits down.)

C: I didn't mean to scare nobody. I'm sorry. Can I stay?

Leader: Yes, only if you can stay seated and talk in a calm voice.

C: Okay.

Leader: How is the rest of the group?

D: I want to share why I'm here.

Leader: Go ahead, and introduce yourself to the group.

D: Oh, yeah, okay. I'm D, and I used to be just like you, C! Angry and (*&^%() like that!

Leader: D, words like that are not appropriate here. Why are you here now, D?

D: I got kicked out of where I was living. I don't have another place to go now. I stopped taking my meds and got manic again. I'm bipolar, they say.

B: This is a good place to get your meds fixed.

Leader *(to B)***:** Thank you for reassuring D. *(to D)* Thank you for your honesty, D. If you want I can find some information for you on bi-polar, but right now we need to hear from the others.

Question 10.4: After reading this scenario, do you believe the leader's opening of the group was effective. If not, what do you think would be a better way to open the group?

The following session is in its 5th week of a 10-week, closed-ended psychoeducational group for teenage girls referred from the Child Protective Services' system focused on peer relations and stress management. Eight girls ranging in age from 14-16 attended.

Leader: Let's do a quick check-in. I want to go around the room and see how everyone's week went. Can you all please fill in the rest of this sentence: "The best thing that happened to me this week was—" Sara, would you start?

Sara: Well, it was a pretty good week. Not the best week I ever had, but not the worst week I ever had either. For me, I finally got my dog to do this trick I was teaching him. My mom thought it was neat too. Also, do you remember that dress I was telling you about before? Well, with my last week's pay check, I was finally able to afford it, and I am so excited.

Mary: That's cool. I saw this horrific movie. But we didn't really watch the movie if you know what I mean. We had a great time in the back of the theatre.

Tina: What theatre did you go to?

Mary: Pallisades—where else? It's the best. My boyfriend and I hang out there all the time.

Sara: That's the worst theatre. I don't know what you like about it.

Mary: What's your problem? Last week you told me that you almost never go to the movies, so how would you even know?

Sara: Yeah, that's only because you can't talk in movies. I mean, what fun is that? Plus they are kind of expensive.

Tina: Oh, you can talk. That's why you sit in the back.

Leader: Okay, everyone, let's get back to our main topic. It sounds like you all have done a great job of finding an activity that you enjoy doing. What do you notice about this activity?

Tina:	It's fun.
Leader:	That's great Tina, what else? What is it that you all notice is going on?
Sara:	I don't understand that question.
Leader:	Is there someone else who can explain it?
Tina:	No.
Leader:	Okay, when you describe this event or activity, such as going to the movies, or playing with your dog, or going shopping, how do you feel?
Tina:	I already told you...it's fun.
Leader:	Right, and does that help you with your stress?
Mary:	Oh yeah, I don't feel stressed while I'm doing it, if that's what you mean.
Leader:	Yes, that's exactly what I mean. It's good to focus on something else when you are feeling stressed. So whenever you are in that stressful situation, whatever it might be, remember that you can draw on your positive experiences and memories.
Mary:	Okay, sounds good. Isn't it time for snack yet?
Leader:	Not quite yet.
Sara:	I'm hungry, too. I want a snack, too.
Tina:	Yeah, snack.
Leader:	First, we are going to break back up into our groups and start working on our clay projects.
Sara:	By the way, when do we finally get to take these home?
Mary:	She already told us we take them home at the end of group. You should listen better.
Leader:	Mary, thank you for your feedback, but is there a different way you could have phrased that to Sara? Do you remember what we have been working on?
Mary:	Okay. *(turns to Sara)* We get to take them home at the end of group.
Leader:	Okay, let's break up into groups now.
Tina:	We really want our snack now.

Question 10.5: After reading this scenario, do you believe the leader's opening of the group was effective. If not, what do you think would be a better way to open the group?

Question 10.6: Recall the scenario with "Katie," the student intern, who took over the group. What was the problem with the opener she used, "Tell me about yourself?" (See Chapter 3.)

An alternative way to start subsequent sessions is to ask as a general question to the group: "What is better this week?" (De Jong et al., 2008). This line of inquiry may begin the group on a positive tone, calling attention to what is going well. This type of opening also sets up the expectation that people will experience change as a result of participating in group and will engender hope that change can happen as one hears others reporting change. There are many other strengths-based openers for groups that can be used when social workers lead open-ended groups in which membership frequently revolves (see openers in Chapter 8 and strengths-based assessment techniques, Chapter 11).

SUMMARY

This chapter has emphasized the importance of formatting sessions with therapeutic ways to draw them to a close and to open sessions with continuing members, as well as when these groups are joined by new members. Some groups have to remain in the beginning stage because of constant revolving membership, but there are still ways to make people's short time in these groups productive. This latter situation is common in the groups social workers may lead in which groups remain in the beginning stage because of open-ended group formats. The suggestions offered here will help social workers make use of this challenge to encourage productive work in group settings.

Chapter 11
Strengths-Based Techniques

A major emphasis of *Groups in Social Work* has been a strengths focus. In this chapter, we will review and encapsulate what you have learned about strengths in prior chapters. We will also offer some further techniques that emphasize the resources that people bring to bear on their problems.

The following list outlines some of the strengths-based techniques that we have covered:

1. Call the group a positive rather than deficit-based name that implies that growth will happen.

2. Use icebreakers, openers, and activities that emphasize strengths (see Chapter 8).

3. Use presuppositional questioning assuming that change will occur (see Chapter 5).

4. Use coping questions (see Chapter 6).

5. Build a vision of a non-problem future (see Chapter 8).

Before we talk about additional strengths-based techniques, consider the following scenarios, which have been discussed throughout the book, and see if you can find a common problem in each of these scenarios that relates to this chapter's topic .

- **Scenario #1**

This group is part of an addiction treatment program for women who are in prison for drug-related offenses. One member, Debra reads her "lifeline" story involving the history of her addiction, which is a required piece of the treatment. Debra has just gotten to the part in her story where she says that she and her siblings trade off care of their children during summers. Debra has said that she spent a lot of time using cocaine and shoplifting during this particular summer.

(Vera raises her hand to make a comment.)

    Vera: I think that they were enabling you. I think you need to look at that. I didn't have anyone to help me. I did it all by myself.

    Debra: That's the way my family works. We would trade off. I get all the kids for two weeks, then my one sister, then the other, then my brother. It ended up that we all got almost the whole summer to ourselves. We still did get-togethers and if the kids wanted to come home, that was okay, but they liked going to their cousins' houses. It was fun for them, and it was like a vacation for all of us.

    Vera: For you, huh! You didn't have to face reality, girl. You got to live in some fantasy world and didn't have to face motherhood like I did. I was here all by myself, no mother, sisters, nothing, not even a husband that was ever home; he was out partying. I think that your family just encouraged you to live a single person's lifestyle, and you didn't face up or own up to your responsibilities. That just gave you more time to shoplift and drug it up.

    Social Worker: I think there may be an alternative way to look at this. I consider that a strength in Debra's life—a supportive family that helps each other.

Vera:	When she was free from children, why wasn't she looking for a job?
Randy:	And they helped each other get high. Wasn't your sister one of the ones that you drugged with?
Vera:	Well, she told us that was a long time ago. Her sister doesn't do drugs no more.
Social Worker:	Debra, would you like to hear Vera's question again?
Debra:	No.

(Silence.)

Debra:	I'm just going to move on.
Vera:	Well, I think that you are in denial about your family enabling you, and I think that you should own up to that.
Social Worker:	I think Debra made it clear she would like to continue with her presentation so we will let her do that. Please continue, Debra.

(Debra continues reading her presentation. The group members make no further comments and at the end when the social worker asks if anyone has feedback for Debra, everyone says no.)

- ### Scenario #2

This excerpt involves an open-ended group called "Relationship Skills" that takes place at a day treatment program for people with chronic mental illness. Group members are doing a worksheet identifying problematic behaviors.

Client #1:	What does the word super-dependence mean? Isn't it good to depend on others? It's not healthy to do everything on your own.
Social Work Intern:	You're right, it's definitely beneficial to rely on others for support. Super-dependency is being overly dependent on someone, not being able to do things for yourself.
Client #1:	Well I depend on my husband for everything. We've been together for 20 years, and he does a lot for me.
Client #2:	It's a sign of weakness to depend on others too much. I am at a point in my life where I only depend on myself. I am the only one I can trust.
Client #1:	Are you saying there is something wrong with me because I depend on my husband a lot? There's nothing wrong with that, *(turning to social work intern)*, is there?
Social Work Intern:	Being able to depend on your spouse is an important part of marriage. It's when you become unable to do things for yourself that the dependency becomes problematic. It is also unhealthy to isolate yourself and not be able to rely on anyone at all.
Client #2:	I think anyone who relies on anyone else is pathetic. It is sick the way some people use their mates for money and other things. I will never make the mistake of marrying again. Worst thing I've ever done.
Social Work Intern:	Client #2, you have some very strong opinions about dependency in quality relationships. What would you like to talk more about with the group?
Client #2:	Nothing. It's really no one else's business about my failed marriage. It's just pathetic though how some people have to rely on others for everything. It's disgusting really.
Client #1:	Who do you think you are? Are you calling me pathetic? My husband and I have been together for a long time. Just because he gives me money, doesn't mean I'm using him. And it doesn't mean I'm super-dependent. I can't believe you have the nerve to say that about me—in front of my face, too. You white girls have no idea what it is like to be a black woman in this city. You just have no idea.

Client #2: Me being white has nothing to do with being too dependent on people. I have made the choice to only depend on myself. That is my personal choice and I have a right to it. Just like you're free to keep your relationship with your husband as it is. It is not my business to tell you that things should change. It's your problem, not mine.

Social Work Intern: Okay, okay, I understand that you both have very important things to add to the group discussion, but I'm going to have to ask you to keep your comments to yourself if you can't respect what others are saying. In order to keep this group a safe place for everyone to voice their ideas and opinions we need to make sure everyone's views are heard and respected. That does not mean you have to agree with them-- just that you respect them.

Client #1: How am I supposed to respect someone who is insulting me in front of my face? I can't believe this B***H! Do you know what I've gone through to get my marriage to where it is today? Did you know he used to hit me? Did you know that? Did you know we used to use together? We'd use and then he'd beat me up. And he has a baby with someone else! Do you know how close to using again I was when I heard that? I've been clean for three months now, and I've been coming here to help me with things. You have no idea how things are for me.

Client #2: I know that you are a pathetic woman if you really think your husband loves you. He's probably cheating on you because he knows how you need him for everything

Social Work Intern: Ladies, there's a better way to handle this. It is inappropriate and absolutely disrespectful to—

Client #1: Whatever! Screw all of you! F*** this place! I'm getting the hell out of here. *(Leaves and slams the door behind her.)*

Client #2: I don't know what her problem is. Sometimes the truth hurts. She just needs to-

Social Work Intern: Please, Client #2. This is not the time to bad mouth Client #1. We can talk about what happened at the break, but right now in front of the rest of the group is not the time.

Client #2: Fine, I don't have anything else to say anyway. (Crosses arms and slumps down for the remainder of the session.)

- ## Scenario #3

In this case, a social work intern was allowed to observe a substance-abuse treatment group for both out-patient and in-patient clients at a psychiatric hospital. Group members are given by names whereas the group leader is indicated as such.

James: I don't even know why I am here. I have no plans of stopping my drinking any time soon.

Dave: Well, you wouldn't have even thought of coming, much less come, if you had no plans of ever quitting.

Matt: I agree.

Sam: Me, too. I was where you were...denial.

James. I'm not in denial. I'm just honest. I'm not like you guys. I have no desire to quit. My dad died a drunk, and he was a good man. So if it is good enough for him, then it is good enough for me.

Matt: Then why are you here?

James: I don't know. This is a waste of time.

Group Leader: What do you mean a waste of time?

James: Have you not been listening? I don't plan on quitting. I don't want to talk about quitting, so this group is then a waste of time. So I'm gonna leave and go home.

Matt:	Come back when you're ready to talk.
Group Leader:	Why don't you stay until the end and listen to the others? We also are giving job training information.
James:	I don't want to listen to anyone else complain. I can go to my sister's house for that.
Group Leader:	No, why don't you go ahead and stay. I think you would really get use out of the job training info.
James:	You think? You don't know me. And if I recall, this is an open-ended group, and I think that means I can leave and come when I want.

(This exchange went back and forth for about five more minutes until James got up and left the group.)

Question 11.1: What problem did you find that was common to each of these scenarios and relates to the topic of this chapter? Write your answer here before reading on.

The problem I saw was that all of these groups were deficit-based. In examining presumed deficits, people either became defensive or were attacking the flaws in others. In the first group, the member hones in on the speaker's "enabling" family, which sets up an impasse in the group and seems to stifle further dialogue. In the second group, the focus is "super-dependency," which leads to a conflict between two members. In the last, one of the group members' focus on "denial" alienates the new member.

STRENGTHS-BASED ASSESSMENT QUESTIONS

One body of strengths-based techniques takes typical assessment questions and phrases them in a way that orients the group members toward the qualities, resources, behaviors, and supports that have helped them show resilience in response to life's challenges (Bertolino & O'Hanlon, 2002). Although I have presented these assessment questions in relation to the type of groups that might make the most use of them, feel free to apply them as appropriate. (Refer to Table 11.1.)

Table 11.1 Strengths-Based Assessment

Domains of Functioning	Types of Groups	Questions
Employment	• Welfare-to-work groups with mothers • Groups of women who may be worried about supporting themselves (e.g., domestic violence victims and non-offending parents of child sexual abuse victims) • Groups with the mentally ill when one of the goals is to obtain employment • Groups with people transitioning from homelessness	• How did you come to work at your current place of employment? • How did you get yourself into position to get the job? • What do you think your employer saw in you that might have contributed to your being hired? • What have you found to be most challenging or difficult about your job? • How have you met or worked toward meeting those challenges and difficulties? • What skills or qualities do you think your employer sees in you? • What qualities do you think you possess that are assets on the job? • (If self-employed) How did you have the means to start your own business? • (If unemployed) What kind of employment would you like to see yourself involved with in the future?
School performance	• Welfare-to-work groups with mothers • Youth with academic problems	• How did you manage to make it through (6th grade, high school, trade school, junior college, a four-year university, two years of college, graduate school, etc.)? • What qualities do you posses that made that happen? • What did you find most challenging about school? • How did you manage any difficulties that you may have encountered while in school? (e.g., completing homework assignments, tests, getting to school on time, moving from one grade to another, teacher/classmates relationships, sports) • In what ways did school prepare you for future challenges?
Interpersonal functioning	• A multitude of groups, particularly people from cultures where the family, kinship ties, and collectivism is valued.	• Who are you closest to in your_____(life, family, etc.)? • What do you appreciate most about your relationship with _____? • What would (he, she, they) say are your best qualities as a _____ (friend, spouse, parent, child, grandparent, colleague, etc.)? • How is it helpful for you to know that? • What does it feel like to know that? • Which relationships have been more challenging for you? How have you dealt with those challenges? • Whom can you go to for help? • Who has made a positive difference in your life? How so? • When are others more helpful to you?
Parenting	• Parenting groups • Welfare-to-work groups • Recovery groups for women with children	• What would your children say about you that makes you a good parent? • When do you think you are able to be your best as a parent? • When do you most enjoy your children? What are you doing then? • How do you deal with parenting challenges? What qualities, behaviors, beliefs, and supports have you draw on? What qualities, behaviors, beliefs, and supports have developed as a result? • How have you done things differently than your parents?
Abuse	• Domestic Violence • Survivors of Sexual Assault • Women in Recovery	• How did you keep yourself safe? • How were you able to leave an abusive situation? • What resilient qualities, behaviors, beliefs and supports did you draw on to survive the abuse? • What qualities, behaviors, beliefs, and supports did you develop as a result of going through the abuse? • How did you decide to be different from the people who hurt you? How have you been able to do this?

 continued on next page...

Table 11.1 Strengths-Based Assessment continued...

Domains of Functioning	Types of Groups	Questions
Previous treatment experience	• Groups with people with severe mental illness	• What did you find helpful about previous therapy? • What did the therapist do that was helpful? How did that make a difference for you? • What wasn't so helpful? • (If currently or previously on psychotropic medication) How was the medication helpful to you? • What, if anything, did the medication allow you to do that you wouldn't have otherwise been able to do? • What qualities do you possess so that you were able to work with the medication to improve things for yourself?
Relapse prevention	• Groups for addictions, mental illness, violence.	• In the past, what kept you from going downhill any further? • How did you manage to bring things to an end? • Who helped you and how did they help you? How might they be helpful to you again? • What signs were there that you were starting to slip? • What can you do next time to be aware of these signs? What will you do when you see those signs? • What have you learned from this experience?

ECO-MAPS TO EMPHASIZE SYSTEMS

An additional strengths-based assessment technique is to have group members complete eco-maps on themselves as a group exercise.[1] This could be conducted as an opening technique when people start the group or any other time as appropriate.

Question 11.2: Why would an eco-map assessment be considered a strengths-based technique? Write your answer here before reading on.

The reason an eco-map is a way to assess strengths is because it highlights the importance of the environment on the functioning of the individual rather than seeing individuals as flawed and dysfunctional. In assessing the context of individual behavior, one can get away from individual pathology as a root cause of the problems that have brought the person to group. Instead, one can focus on developing the environmental supports needed to bolster an individual's functioning.

[1] Most social work students are familiar with the eco-map assessment from introductory courses, so we will not go into here. However, one may find the following website helpful for constructing eco-maps: http://www.gingerich.net/courses/SSWM517/ecomap.pdf

REFRAMING

Reframing involves giving people credit for the positive aspects of their behavior (Berg, 1994), casting their motives in a benevolent light (Morris, Alexander, & Waldron, 1988), or introducing a novel way of viewing some aspect of themselves, others, their problem, or situation (Bertolino & O'Hanlon, 2002). A new perspective on the problem can generate new actions in accordance with this frame of reference.

1. Recall the example of the substance abuse treatment group for women at the prison (see page 65). One of the group members interrupts Debra's "lifeline" story to tell her that she thinks Debra's family enabled her addiction. The social worker offers a reframe of what one group member views as negative (enabling) to a positive attribute (supportive).

2. The following example, involving physical abuse, emphasizes the positive intention behind potentially harmful behaviors. When parents physically abuse their children, they often have positive intentions, such as wanting their children to behave, to be responsible about chores, and to perform well in school. The positive intention behind the discipline can be emphasized without condoning the negative behavior. Instead, the focus of intervention will be on how parents can meet the same intentions with positive behaviors.

A "reframing" exercise was used in a group for juvenile offenders. They were asked to take the illegal behavior for which they had become involved with the juvenile justice system and draw a picture of that behavior being used in a positive way. One youth had been in trouble for auto theft; he now pictured his mechanical abilities being used to fix cars. Another boy, on probation for "tagging" graffiti art, showed himself drawing and expressing himself through his art. These examples illustrate how the group members sought out the positive attributes in their negative behaviors.

EXCEPTION-FINDING

Exception-finding, focusing on when the problem is better (or not as bad) is one of the main interventions of solution-focused therapy (De Jong et al., 2008). Exception-finding serves a number of purposes. First, it helps people discover the resources and supports they already utilize. Second, inquiry about times when the situation is better reduces the tendency of people to experience the problem as overwhelming or all-encompassing. A student intern illustrates the use of exception-finding in a substance abuse treatment group at a state hospital. The session was on "triggers" for use. At the end of that discussion she asked, "Tell me about a time when one of the triggers happened, and you didn't use. What did you do during that time?" The first group member talked about wanting to keep his job so he could make child support payments.

Social Work Intern: Has anyone else not used for similar reasons?

Susan: Yeah, I can relate. I have two kids and one that CPS already took because of my using. I can remember one time I was on the street and had my last bit of money. I was going to give it to the dope man, but something in me just stopped. I had a picture of my daughter in my mind, and I knew she needed food. So I went on home.

Social Work Intern:	So it sounds like, for both of you, your children were big factors in stopping you from using on that occasion. How about the rest of you?
Robert:	I didn't use one time because my mom was in the hospital, and I knew if I used I would never go see her. The doctors said it was serious, and I didn't want her to die and never see her again. So I went to the hospital, and I was real glad I did.
Social Work Intern:	What about going to the hospital made you feel good?
Robert:	It was just seeing my mom's face when I walked in the door. She was really happy to see me. Now I did go out and use right after that, but not before.
Social Work Intern:	Can you see any common themes in what kept you all from using?
Susan:	Family members—kids, mom.
Social Work Intern:	What can we learn from that?
Susan:	That family is real important and people count on us.
Robert:	We're supposed to be responsible.
John:	It's important because they love us.
Social Work Intern:	So how might knowing that family members count on you and love you help you the next time you want to use?
John:	Just remembering their faces sometimes gets me through.
Social Work Intern:	How about the rest of you? What do you think?
Susan:	Sometimes if I just concentrate real hard on thinking about my baby and how I really do want a better life for her and I don't want her to go down the same path I went; that helps me.
Social Work Intern:	So it sounds like for all of you, a family member in need played a big part. John, your son needed child support. Susan, your daughter needed food. Robert, your mom needed to see you when she was sick. All of you said earlier that using drugs makes you feel like a loner, but you've all described people in your lives that really need you and love you. So maybe if we can work on building the relationships with the people that matter most to you, perhaps you can find ways to feel more connected and not so alone.
Group Members:	Yeah, that makes sense.

In this example, group members identified reasons that they refrained from using. At the end, the leader identified the exceptions (related to relationships with others) that they could perhaps enlarge upon to help them even further in their efforts to abstain.

The opening activity the "self-esteem group" at the adolescent psychiatric unit was for the members was to rate their self-esteem on a scale of 1 to 10 before they entered the facility and then again at present.

Kailey:	Oh, an eight now. I guess a six before I came in.
Juliana:	Maybe a four now. Like a one when I came in.
Zach:	A seven before, maybe a four now.
Chase:	I have like NO self-esteem. A zero when I came in; a zero now. There's just nothing there.
Reina:	You should have more than that! After what I told you Candy said?

Chase:	But my self-esteem is about what I think about me.
Kailey:	You should feel good after what Jill said last group.
Juliana:	And what I said to you just before this group.
Chase:	But it's about me, about how I feel about myself. That's just zero.
Facilitator:	Okay, Amaya?
Amaya:	I think I have a six now, probably a two when I came in.

(After that, the group interactions evolved into discussions about their family lives and the abuse most of them had suffered.)

This example, in which clients merely rate their self-esteem, shows the importance of asking clients what resources and supports they have used and the qualities they possess that enabled them to move forward on the scale. This conversation would have been more empowering for the teens if they would have been pushed to identify what they have learned to feel better. The group member, Chase, made a good point when he said that his self-esteem represents what he feels about himself rather than what other people tell him. This is why exception-finding involves inquiry of group members as to what is different, rather than telling people their strengths. You can get people to elaborate upon their strengths by investigating the circumstances using *who* (Who is there when the exception occurs? What are they doing differently? What would they say you are doing differently?), *what* (What was happening before? What is different about the behavior? What happens afterwards? What are you thinking to make this happen?), *where* (Where is the exception occurring? How does the place help?), *when* (How often is this happening? What time of the day is it?), and *how* questions (How are you making this happen? What strengths/talents/qualities are you drawing upon?).

Consider the following scenario in an open-ended support group for people in early recovery. Ten members are present—seven men and three women. Answer the question that follows.

Facilitator:	Good evening everyone, please welcome Peter to group. Would someone tell Peter how we introduce new members to group?
Beth:	We usually ask new members questions, Peter, like why are you here?
Peter:	I had a busy weekend using and I went through $20,000. I own a restaurant and now I don't have money for paychecks. My wife told me if I didn't get help she would leave me.
Eric:	What's your drug of choice? That's a lot of money.
Peter:	Coke. Yeah, I shared it around.
Eric:	That would have paid off my student loans!
Facilitator:	Any other questions for Peter?
Ann:	Do you drink too?
Peter:	Only when I'm coming off of coke, but it's not a problem.
Buddy:	Yeah, alcohol never was a problem for me either, but now I understand that you can be cross-addicted to anything. Drinking alcohol led me back to my drug of choice, so be aware that it could happen to you too.
Peter:	Well, I doubt that, but I guess I am open to anything.
Beth:	Well, I have been doing drugs since high school and I have never had problems with alcohol.

Facilitator:	Any other questions for Peter?
Elizabeth:	You know, I have a lot of trouble with all this stuff...cross-addiction...the 12-steps...I mean, (to leader) you aren't in recovery, are you?

(Silence)

Elizabeth:	I mean, it's easy for everyone who works here to say what you can and can not do, but unless you are in our situation, how can you say what is right for us?
Facilitator:	Okay, I take it that we are ready to move the discussion from Peter. Is everyone okay with that—or are there any other questions for Peter?
Eric:	No, but welcome to group, man.
Peter:	Thanks.
Elizabeth :	*(To the leader)* Could you answer my question now?
Facilitator:	I've been running group therapies for about 15 years now and I don't discuss my personal issues. I know that frustrates some clients, but the focus needs to be on your recovery.
David:	Well, this group has been helpful to me regardless of whether you are in recovery or not. I'm grateful for these groups and that is why I'm a bit nervous about leaving today.
Ann:	I don't know if I am ready to leave later this week. I had dinner with a friend this week, and she was pressuring me to have one drink. I tried to explain the program, but she wouldn't take no for an answer. I managed to leave, but I don't think we'll be friends since I wouldn't drink with her.
Buddy:	I had trouble with some friends too, but I had an old girlfriend come back into my life and say that she is proud of me, so I'm just not going to let the guys who don't understand get me in trouble.
Eric:	I want to go back to what Elizabeth was saying about AA meetings. I got in trouble with Dorothy (program director) because I couldn't make three meetings last week because of work. I think it's easy for you guys to tell us what to do, but you aren't trying to work too. I mean, this is your job!
Facilitator:	Well, Eric and Elizabeth seem pretty frustrated with the program rules; is anyone else having trouble with following the contract that you signed at admission?
Ann:	Well, last time I was in the program I didn't follow the rules and look where it got me. So, this time I decided that I had better do what I was told.
Peter:	You were here before?
Ann:	Yes, last year. I wasn't ready then, but I think that I am now. It is difficult, though, especially when friends act like the one did this week.
Facilitator:	I hear that some of you are frustrated and fearful. I also know that most of you drank or used to bury these feelings in the past, so congratulations on making different choices here tonight and for your futures.

Question 11.3: What opportunity presents itself for exception-finding? When you have identified it, what type of questions would you ask?

An example of the need to explore exceptions is represented in a PTSD treatment group in which members talked about feeling on edge and agitated. When they were asked about when they felt a bit more relaxed, one group member said that watching television distracted him from his thoughts. Another talked about coloring with his daughter.

> Mike: I was annoyed at first when she handed me some crayons, but then the longer I colored, the more relaxed I felt.
>
> Leader: Is this something you would be willing to do more often—coloring with your daughter?

Question 11.4: In this scenario, what do you think of the way the leader responded to the "exception"? Is there anything you would have done differently?

SUMMARY

This chapter has focused on strengths-based techniques, namely ways to orient assessment questions towards strengths, reframing, and exception-finding. This chapter has continued the emphasis in this workbook on strengths-based techniques. Social work group facilitators can demonstrate competence in eliciting and cultivating strengths and resources in group participants because it will help empower group members and will offer them hope. An enhanced view of themselves and the problem will most likely lead to increased motivation and to change.

Chapter 12
Cognitive-Behavioral Interventions

Cognitive-behavioral approaches derive philosophically, theoretically, and empirically from four theories of learning: respondent conditioning (associative learning), operant conditioning (the effect of the environment, particularly reinforcement and punishment, on patterns of behavior), observational learning (learning by imitation), and cognitive learning (the impact of thought patterns on feelings and behavior) (Corcoran, 2006). They combine to provide a broad class of present-focused interventions with a shared focus on changing *cognition* (thoughts, beliefs, and assumptions about the world), changing *behavior*, and building clients' *coping skills.* Appendix I lists many curricula resources and among these are cognitive-behavioral group interventions, which will provide more detail about application to particular populations and problems. Although the focus of this workbook is not on running cognitive-behavioral groups, facilitators can familiarize themselves with certain cognitive-behavioral interventions that underlie many groups, even if they are not identified as such.

BEHAVIORAL REINFORCEMENT SYSTEMS

Groups can be structured with the use of behavioral interventions, in which reinforcers are used to encourage compliance with group rules and participation. This is most often done with children who may have difficulty with their behavior, such as children with aggression, defiance or impulsivity. In-patient facilities, such as hospitals and residential treatment programs that house youth, often have a strict behavioral program in place in which certain behaviors earn points and privileges. These behavioral systems cover attendance and behavior in group treatment, which is frequently the dominant modality of treatment in such settings.

As a social work intern, I co-led two groups of preschool children (one group of three year olds and one group of four year olds) who had been maltreated. A loose behavioral structure was in place for these young children; they were told that as long as they minded, they would receive a reward (a small toy chosen from a box) at the end of group. If children misbehaved, they were redirected. If that did not work, they were warned about possibly not earning their reward at the end of group unless they changed their behavior. During the semester I co-led these two groups, only one child did not get his reward for the group.

Other groups might be more tightly structured. For instance, at the same agency, I co-led a group for school-aged maltreated boys. My co-leader awarded a point every time a boy made an appropriate response in group. At the end, the highest scorer was given a small prize of his choosing.

In hindsight, my co-facilitator and I should have organized the group around a behavioral system. As discussed, we had difficulty managing the acting-out behaviors of the boys, which might have been due to the range of ages represented in the group and their discomfort with the topic. During one particular session, my co-leader and I lost control of the group. The boys ran, not only out of the group room, but also in front of their mothers who were waiting in the reception area, outside the building. As they chased each other around on the lawn, my co-leader and I futilely tried to corral the boys back into group. At the time, I was mortified. My only consolation was that my co-leader (a six-foot-two male) was no more able to influence the boys than I. Now I see the humor in the situation, but it was definitely one of those "worst group moments." The lesson here (in addition to making sure that the boys' ages were closer) was to use a behavior system that reinforces compliance and participation. Perhaps, then we would have been able to maintain better control over the group and the group would have met its purpose.

Question 12.1: How could the use of a behavioral system have helped the functioning of this group? How would you have devised such a system?

A further example of a behavioral system, this time with adults, can be seen in the sex offender group first discussed on pages 62-63. In this group, participation and progress on the "steps" was linked to a positive report to the group members' probation officers.

Question 12.2: How could the use of a behavioral system have helped the functioning of this group? How would you have devised such a system?

COMMUNICATION SKILLS

People often attend groups because of problems in interpersonal functioning. Additionally, people within group might experience conflict among themselves, especially when members spend time together outside the group as in residential treatment settings, hospitals, schools, prison settings, and when groups progress into the middle stage of group development (see Chapter 7). Therefore, teaching group members about communication skills provides them with an invaluable asset they can use in all aspects of their lives. The group context is particularly helpful because members can learn a lot from seeing skills modeled by the leader(s), practicing the skills with each other, and learning from other people's efforts.

Briefly outlined here are the steps for communication skill training. Although they will be described in rote fashion, recall the guidelines for presenting information in a collaborative way.

Relay why communication skills are important

- To initiate new relationships.
- To build or maintain already-existing relationships.
- To experience closeness with others.
- To state feelings and reactions to let others know of their influence and to get them to act more positively.
- To cope with feelings by sharing them with others.

Teach reflective listening

- Explain what reflective listening means: paraphrasing the content of the speaker's message and one's perceptions of the underlying feelings in order to convey understanding of the speaker's message. To do this, use the basic format: "What I hear you saying . . ." or "You seem to be feeling [mad, sad, scared, glad, etc.] because [give brief reason]." Generally, the most difficulty people have with this technique is understanding that reflective listening does not mean they necessarily agree with the speaker's message. Rather, it conveys understanding to ensure that the other person feels heard.

Question 12.3: Refer to the scenario of the group held at the acute psychiatric unit involving Marcus and Harold (pages 57-58). Do you think that it would be worth having a unit in this group on reflective listening? How would you teach such material with this population? How could you get the group to make a reflective listening statement in reaction to what Marcus has said?

Teach "I" messages

- Present the basic format: I feel (personal reactions) to what happened (a specific activating event).
- To practice, group members can be asked to come up with a situation in which they need to communicate a negative feeling to a person in their lives. In "round robin"

style, group members, without going into the details of their situation, are asked to compose an "I" message. These are written down by the facilitator so statements can be examined more closely. Some will have to be revised as they will be nothing more than disguised "you statements" (e.g., "I feel that you lied," rather than "I feel disappointed that you didn't tell me the truth"). Group members gain practice in the skill by helping other members construct appropriate statements.

<u>Asking people to change their behavior</u>

* Sometimes when people use "I" messages, they want nothing more than to be heard. At other times, however, they would like others to change their behavior. Group members are taught that requests should be behaviorally specific, measurable, and stated as the presence of positive behaviors.

The following excerpt from a psychoeducational, closed-ended group for court-ordered domestic violence offenders illustrates some of these skills.

Facilitator: Last week we started talking about communication skills, including the use of "I" statements. Let's hear from someone who tried this out over the last week.

Jim: Yeah, I tried it but can't say it went any better than usual, which is to say pretty bad.

Facilitator: Could you tell us about the situation and what was said?

Jim: Sure. I told Melissa I resent always being the one to have to wash the car just because she never does. Then she goes all ballistic, said something like she didn't give a damn about the f'ing car—and things went rapidly downhill from there. So much for "I" statements.

Facilitator: *(turning to the rest of the group)* What do you think? How might Jim have worded this differently and possibly gotten a more positive reaction from Melissa?

Carlos: Man, that's not the way you talk to your woman. We learned that. For starters she probably got all riled up because you said she never washes the car. That's an attack, man, and she didn't like it.

Jim: So how would you have said it?

Carlos: Telling her how you feel was a good start. How about something like, "Melissa, I feel resentful because it seems like I'm always the one washing the car." I gather from what she said that washing the car isn't high on her list of priorities? That's fair to say, right?

Jim: Yea, I'm sure it isn't nowhere on her list of priorities.

Carlos: Then, how about if you say that and be happy if she just helps out a little? What if you say, "I know a clean car is more important to me than to you, but how about if out of three months, you wash it one month and I wash it two? I'd really appreciate that. It would mean a lot to me." What do you think of that?

Jim: Yeah, that might have gone down better.

Facilitator: Carlos, you made some good suggestions, and they included the main points we talked about last week. Who can tell us what particular communication skills Carlos used in rephrasing this request?

Dan:	He didn't accuse his wife of doing anything wrong.
Facilitator:	Good. Yes, that's very important. What else?
Jim:	The request is put into specific and measurable terms. I'd ask her to wash the car— that's specific—and every third month—that's measurable.
Facilitator:	You got it! And the final thing we talked about? *(pause)* Anyone? Okay, Jim's request is for a <u>positive</u> behavior. He's asking Melissa to do something positive, not to stop doing something negative.
Alex:	Well, my kid drives me nuts 'cause he's constantly standing up on his chair when we're eating even though I've told him a thousand times not to. So how do I tell him in a "positive" way not to stand up?
Facilitator:	How old is your son, Alex?
Alex:	He's five.
Facilitator:	Does anyone have any ideas for Alex?
Jim:	Even if he's five, you want to be respectful. I'd ask him to sit down when you're eating.
Facilitator:	That's a good answer, Jim. Yes, parents can be respectful and authoritative at the same time. So putting that into a command might sound like "Bobby (or whatever his name is), I need you to sit in your chair when we're eating." It's positive—telling him what to do—not what not to do, and it's specific and measurable. What other tools did we talk about that could be very helpful with children?
Dan:	A behavioral reinforcement system?
Facilitator:	Absolutely! How might you plan and implement it?
Dan:	You could give a sticker or some other reward every time he sits down throughout the entire dinner. Maybe if he has enough stickers at the end of the week, he could pick something special to do with his parents, or pick his favorite meal for Saturday night, something that would make him really happy.
Facilitator:	Those are great ideas, and that's exactly how a behavioral reinforcement system works. I'd just add that as soon as he starts to stand up, remind him that if he remains seated, he'll get a sticker or a reward. One more important point, because of his age, eye contact and touch are important in communicating. So hold both of his hands and look him directly in the eyes, make your request, then ask him to repeat back what you said. It's much more likely that he'll remember what you say if you do this. Does that make sense?
Alex:	Sure, it's worth a try, even if it means eating Mac and Cheese on Saturday nights.

PROBLEM-SOLVING

As discussed, people naturally fall into telling others what to do, even though in group, the general guideline is to avoid premature advice-giving. Instead, the emphasis is on listening and helping people express their feelings and clarifying their thoughts about a situation, so that people can reach a new understanding of their situation and can ultimately reach some resolution of the problem. The problem-solving process comprises of five steps (Beach et al., 1990; D'Zurilla & Nezu, 1999; Christensen, Wheeler, & Jacobsen, 2007):

- Defining the problem
- Brainstorming
- Evaluating the alternatives
- Choosing and implementing an alternative
- Evaluating the implemented option

Teaching people how to solve their own problems is an important skill, and a group is an excellent venue for problem-solving because there are so many people to generate ideas. Additionally, problem-solving therapy, a type of cognitive-behavioral treatment characterized by the problem-solving process, has been associated with improved mental and physical adjustment (Malouff, Thorsteinsson, & Schutte, 2007).

The steps of the problem-solving process will be illustrated with Dara, a person attending a depression treatment group. Dara complained of feeling very lonely after her husband had left her. She had started working as a secretary at an office, but didn't like her new job.

Defining the problem: Break down complex problems so you can tackle only one problem at a time, and define the problem in behavioral terms. Dara said she hated her new job. When asked what specific part of it she hated most, she responded that she felt excluded by the other office workers. With further prompting, she decided that lunchtime was the worst because she didn't have anyone to go to lunch with, and she felt excluded by the other three secretaries, who either went out to a local restaurant or ate with each other in the cafeteria. The problem definition therefore became, "What should Dara do at lunchtime"?

Brainstorming: Generate and write down all possible solutions, even those that seem impossible or silly. Encourage spontaneity and creativity by prohibiting critical comments. Consider the following angles on which to brainstorm:

- changing the environment (e.g., moving residences or changing jobs, filing a complaint about environmental conditions, hiring a babysitter to handle parenting stress);

- reframing the problem (finding a different way to look at it);

- changing the interaction patterns around a problem (doing something different instead of having the same arguments);

- coping with it (telling yourself a job is worth putting up with for now because you want a good reference when you look for a new job in six months);

- asking relationship questions (What would other people say about how to solve the problem?);

- reflecting on what has worked with similar situations in the past (previous problem-solving attempts)?

For Dara's lunchtime situation, the group members came up with the following ideas:

> - *Ask the other office workers if she could join them*
> - *Invite one or more of the secretaries to join her for lunch*
> - *Invite someone outside of the secretarial pool to join her for lunch*
> - *Change jobs*
> - *Change departments (another building)*
> - *Work through lunch and hopefully get a raise*
> - *Run errands during lunchtime*
> - *Join a gym and work out at lunch*
> - *Go for a walk at lunch and listen to her iPod*
> - *Work on a hobby*
> - *Play computer games*
> - *Read a book and eat lunch at her desk*
> - *Call the other group members at lunchtime to get support*
> - *Complain to her boss*

Evaluating the alternatives: After patently irrelevant or impossible items are crossed out, discuss the advantages and disadvantages of each remaining viable alternative. Viable possibilities from Dara's perspective included changing jobs, running errands, walking during lunch, and calling other group members.

Choosing and implementing an alternative: After the number of options has been narrowed down, select one or more strategies that seem to maximize benefits over costs, and practice skills that might be necessary to successfully implement the solution.

> *Dara decided that she would leave the office and run errands or go for a walk. She said she needed to lose weight anyway so the latter would be helpful in this regard. She was relieved and pleased to find out other group members would be available for support during lunchtime by phone. She said she didn't want to "risk" inviting anyone out for lunch at her office, but agreed to role play the situation in group at a later time.*

Evaluate the implemented option: Explore "failures" to see which elements went well and which ones need further work. Perhaps select another option from the list. At the next session, Dara said that after she started going out at lunch to run errands or take a walk, that, funnily enough, she had been invited to join the other secretaries to eat lunch in the cafeteria. The other group members commented that perhaps it was because she had acted as if she was not dependent upon their invitation that had caused them to open their ranks to her.

ROLE PLAYING

Groups are an excellent modality when peoples problems are due to their interpersonal functioning. People tend to learn how to interact with others by watching other people (modeling) or by practicing new behaviors (behavioral rehearsal) process called role playing. Toseland and Rivas (2009) argue that group facilitators do not make available use of role playng because of:

- Its contrived nature
- Initial reluctance of some members to role playing
- The extra instructions and direction the facilitator has to provide to make the role play work
- The facilitator has to be adept in the particular behavior in order to perform as a model for members

Question 12.4: For each reason described by Toseland and Rivas as to why group leaders do not have group members practice new behaviors, provide some counter-arguments and/or suggestions to overcome these potential barriers.

The following steps are suggested for role playing (Hepworth et al., 2006).

- **<u>Group leader models skills</u>**

The group leaders (or the leader and the client wanting to try out a new behavior) demonstrate the skill so that the clients can experience what it looks like. When the "client role" is demonstrated, he/she first plays the *other role* and then subsequently plays him/herself. In this way, pressure is reduced on the client and taking on another role introduces a note of playfulness and humor to a situation that may have been previously viewed with grim seriousness.

- **<u>Discuss the modeling in group</u>**

The group members provide feedback on the role play and verbalize what was different as a result of the new interaction pattern. The group leader can respond to any questions.

- **<u>The group member behaviorally rehearses the new skill</u>.**

The group member practices the new behavior with either the leader or (even better) a volunteer from the group. This process enables parts of the skill that were unclear or that were misunderstood to come to light for clarification. When the group member tries the new behavior, the chances of him or her being able to generalize the behavior to a real-life situation are increased.

- **The group processes the behavioral rehearsal.**

The group member expresses what it was like to try on the new behavior. Other group members then offer compliments on areas that went well and feedback for improvement, if necessary. Depending on the group, the leader might want to structure responses so that positive statements emerge, for example, "Let's start with what went well. Can you name three things?" (Toseland & Rivas, 2009). Potential barriers and challenges are further discussed.

COGNITIVE RESTRUCTURING

This workbook will cover the technique of cognitive restructuring because so often people in group talk about distorted (also called "negative," "irrational," or "unrealistic") thinking or beliefs that get in their way of functioning. Being able to tackle such beliefs, therefore, is an important skill for group workers. The tasks of cognitive restructuring, which we will address, are: 1) Educate the client about the connection between thoughts, feelings, and behaviors; 2) Identify the thoughts, 3) Examine the validity of the beliefs, and 4) Substitute the thoughts.

Groups pose an advantage for addressing distorted thinking because group members are often able to provide different possibilities and perspectives than a member who is caught in the grip of limiting beliefs. Additionally, people are often able to hear such perspectives from their peers much more easily than they do from an authority figure (the leader) who they may see as different from themselves.

Because it is not uncommon for group leaders from different theoretical perspectives (not just a cognitive-behavioral orientation) to address unrealistic thinking, two different methods will be presented—one less structured, primarily calling on the group members to offer different perspectives and the other more educational in nature.

The following example is drawn from a men's addiction recovery group held at a halfway house. George, who is on probation, and fearful of having to go to jail should he violate the terms of his probation, summarizes a recent meeting with his probation officer then states, "It's like they're out to get me looking for a reason to throw me in jail, and with my bad luck I'm sure they'll find something to get me on."

By allowing George to see that he has choices, and that his outcome rests on his own efforts and choices, he might feel a heightened sense of responsibility, but it also offers hope and a sense of empowerment that he can direct events to be different in the future. Furthermore, by hearing from others who have struggled to make difficult choices, and have seen some benefit from doing so, George can see that it might be possible to actually make the necessary changes.

This method shows how the group leader, if attuned to the impact of distorted thinking on feelings and behavior, can pull in the other group members so they can offer a group member struggling with self-limiting beliefs different ways of viewing the problem and hearing feedback on the way he comes across. This is one way to challenge distorted thinking in groups.

Leader:	What do others hear George expressing?
Member #1:	You're sounding like you're the victim, but you made the choices that landed you on probation, not bad luck.
Leader:	Does anyone else hear that?
Member #2:	It sounds like you're saying it's out of your hands. Like there's nothing you can do to avoid going to jail, but if you follow the requirements, you won't have to, right?
George:	But they think this is the way to do it; to keep me on track by threatening me?
Leader:	Your probation officer can do anything he wants, but you're the one who makes the choice of how to respond. You can respond negatively and deal with the consequences or you can react positively in a way that will keep you out of jail.
George:	But it always seems that something ends up happening and I get in trouble.
Leader:	Does something just happen or do you make choices? What does everyone else think?
Member #3:	I used to think things just happened to me too—bad luck—and that everyone was against me. But if you try something different, you might not have so much bad luck.
George:	But it's always been this way, I never get any breaks, I can't just make them happen.
Leader:	What does everyone hear in the language George uses?
Member #4:	Always; never; can't.
Member #1:	Self-defeating. It's like you don't even give yourself a chance. You're already telling yourself this is the way it has to be. You're talking yourself into a situation you don't have to choose.

(George nods but is silent.)

Leader:	You're nodding. Does that mean you can identify with what was just said?
George:	I guess I'm just scared.
Leader:	I'm sure there are others who are scared in this room.
Member #2:	I'm scared all the time about doing something stupid, but it's only me who makes that choice, no one else.

An alternative, more aligned with cognitive-behavioral interventions, offers a formal process of cognitive restructuring. This process involves four steps (Corcoran, 2006):

- Educating the client about the connection between thoughts and feelings
- Identifying the thoughts
- Examining the validity of the beliefs
- Replacing the irrational or problematic thoughts with more functional thoughts.

Educate the Client About the Connection between Thoughts, Feelings, and Behaviors

The first step in cognitive restructuring is to educate the client on the connection between thoughts, feelings, and behaviors with statements such as, "Let's take a look at what you've been saying to yourself. Are you aware that your mind is constantly generating messages? These thoughts we're having influence how we feel and act, even though we might not be very aware of them at first. But we actually have more control over these than you might think, and it is one way that we can directly influence the way we feel and act."

An example is sometimes helpful for people to further understand the connection between feelings, thoughts, and actions. For example, if a person feels depressed, she may not feel like getting out of bed. Staying in bed (the behavior) may then cause her to feel even worse (she is not getting done what she needs to and consequently feels worse about herself). Thoughts and actions are also inter-related in the same way. For example, if the same person thinks, "I don't feel like getting up, but staying in bed is just going to make me feel worse. I'm going to get up and get stuff done. That will probably help." These types of thoughts might result in her getting out of bed and accomplishing tasks and may, in turn, influence the thoughts she's having (i.e., "Now that I'm up, it doesn't seem so bad. At least I'm getting stuff done."). She, in turn, may experience a boost in mood.

In a group for mothers of sexual-abuse victims, the group facilitator provides the example of a woman who gets a flat tire on the way to the work (Corcoran, 2004). Her thoughts are: "Nothing ever works out for me. The whole day is ruined. I'm going to be late for work now, and I'll probably get fired. I don't know what I'm going to do. I can't stand this."

When the facilitator asks, "How would you feel if you had these thoughts?", group members are able to see that this pattern of thinking could lead to negative feelings such as depression, helplessness, and anxiety.

The facilitator contrasts the same situation with the flat tire but with a different set of thinking patterns: "Well, this is inconvenient getting a flat tire, but it happens to everyone every once in awhile. It's lucky I'm only five blocks away from a garage. I can walk there and get help. I can also call work to tell them what happened. I'll be late. I don't like that this happened, but I'll be able to take care of it." Group members can see that the alternative response is more likely to lead to problem-solving attempts and coping rather than hopelessness, dejection, and stress.

Identify the Thoughts

After educating the client, the next step involves helping group members identify the thoughts preceding and accompanying the distressing emotions and non-productive action ("What was going through your mind...?"). In the group with the mothers of sexual-abuse victims, one of the members, Miranda, has had her children placed into foster care (Corcoran, 2003). Miranda says she misses her daughters and wants them back, but doesn't know how to make it without her husband. She says, "I was a single parent for a little while—six months—and it was the worst time of my life. I had a hard time finding work because all I had was a G.E.D. I ended up at a fast-food restaurant, which was totally humiliating with all these kids working there. I was always struggling, and couldn't pay my bills. We lived in this crappy apartment, and I could never get the landlord to fix anything. Now we live in a house, and my husband makes good money as a plumber. What am I going to do if I'm alone again? And this time I'd have two kids to take care of, not just one. I want my daughters back with me, but without him I don't think I can make it."

The facilitator asks the group to help Miranda name her unrealistic thoughts, providing the hint that words such as "never" "always," and other absolutist language are usually signals. Some group members have difficulty differentiating thoughts and feelings; some confuse facts ("I was a single parent for six months") for unrealistic thoughts. Group members start to catch on though as the unrealistic thoughts are named correctly and listed on a flip chart: "What am I going to do if I'm alone again?" "Without him I don't think I can make it." "I could never get the landlord to fix anything."

Miranda defends her thoughts, insisting, "But they're all true." The facilitator says that while thoughts can seem very convincing, that doesn't necessarily mean they're true. If they're producing negative emotions (helplessness, confusion) and behaviors (staying with her husband and allowing her children to live in foster care), then they need to be questioned.

Examine the Validity of the Beliefs

After the beliefs have been identified, they are examined for their validity. The different ways of doing this include examining the evidence for the belief, considering an alternative perspective ("What's a different way to view this?"); looking at the worst-case scenario ("What's the worst that can happen?"); point-counterpoint (examining the advantages and the disadvantages of the belief); didactic teaching (giving people information that will help them change their beliefs); and experiential learning, by helping clients set up natural experiments so they can test the extent to which their beliefs about an event are unrealistic. (See Corcoran, 2006).

A group is a helpful place for examining beliefs because of the many perspectives and experiences offered by the different members. Additionally, we have already mentioned the tendency of many group members to be able to take in feedback from their peers that they are not able to hear from professionals. In the mothers of sexual-abuse victims group, the members challenge Miranda's belief that she won't be able to make it without her partner because many of the members are making it on their own—albeit not easily. Octavia says, "Me and my little girl had to move out of my parents' house, and that was hard, because the reason I moved in with them is because I didn't have any money. My ex left me with all these debts. I still have his debts to pay, and we're just staying with a cousin of mine right now. It's hard, but it's better than my little girl getting abused."

"I just don't think I could handle what you're going through," Miranda says.

"It's worth it. Because I know what I'm doing is right," Octavia says, "no one has ever stood up to my dad before. All my life he did whatever he wanted to all of us and my mother let him. Finally, I'm standing up to that and it feels real good."

Demetria says she is staying in a transitional living program for homeless women because her family members are worse off than she is. She says it's hard living among a bunch of women "who can't control their kids" and sharing space with people who "don't know how to act." But she also says that the program has a lot to offer in the way of job training, vocational guidance, and assistance with housing.

Substitute the Thoughts

The final step in cognitive restructuring is to substitute the unrealistic beliefs with thinking that is more functional. With the group's help, Miranda comes up with the belief, "I can make it with my girls on my own without my husband."

Miranda admits to feeling a bit better, as if her situation is not as hopeless. The facilitator instructs that by continuing to target and challenge inaccurate thoughts and beliefs, distressing emotions will be ameliorated and changed into more positive feelings.

SUMMARY

This chapter has conveyed some of the basic cognitive-behavioral techniques that might be of value in different group interventions. Helping people communicate more effectively, solve their problems in a more efficient way, and to identify and correct their distorted thinking are skills that many group interventions attempt to effect in their members. If the reader wants more in-depth information about cognitive-behavioral interventions in groups, he or she is encouraged to consult Bieling et al. (2006) or any of the cognitive-behavioral curriculums listed in Appendix 1.

Chapter 13
Handling Difficult Group Member Behaviors

People display some characteristic behaviors when they operate in groups. A Few may dominate and try to take the group over; such members may also have a flair for the dramatic. On the other side, some people hardly talk at all. Others sidetrack the group with their humor. The following sections will be named after the type of roles certain behaviors describe (Corey et al., 1992). However, leaders must not use these labels with group members; the focus of any discussion should be on individuals' behaviors. This chapter will also help you, as the group leader, how to face these patterns, which typically arise in group dynamics.

OVERALL STRATEGY

The initial strategy is to first set up group guidelines (see Chapter 4), so that you can refer back to them as needed. For example, "I want to remind everyone that we want equal participation in the group [established guidelines], and we want to hear from those who have not yet had a chance to share yet today."

If reminders do not work, the group leader may initiate a discussion of the problem behavior. The group leader may start by asking the person to describe his or her behavior: "What do you notice is happening right now with you? What are you doing? How do you think you're coming off in the group?" Then have the other members describe their perception of the person's behavior and their reactions to it, cultivating responsibility for everyone's reactions to the role behavior (Toseland & Rivas, 2009). After all, members are allowing the behaviors to continue if they do not challenge them. As Yalom states, "The client always abides in a dynamic equilibrium with a group that permits or encourages such behavior" (Yalom, 1985, p. 393). Possible advantages for group member abdication of responsibility are that they then assume little accountability for the therapeutic goals of the group; they may have fears of assertiveness or harming the person with the problem behavior; and/or they enjoy being a member of the victimized majority.

When giving feedback, group members are told to speak from an "I" position ("John, I feel frustrated when I have something that's important for me to talk about, and we run out of time because you keep talking."). In order to respond honestly, group members must possess confidence that the group leader will protect them if the original member reacts defensively or in anger. Group leaders will also have to monitor the amount of feedback that the original member receives, so as not to overwhelm or alienate that person.

Once group members have shared, the group leader can ask the original member about his or her reactions to the feedback and whether this is a pattern that the person experiences in other aspects of his or her life. The person will also be asked if he or she wants to experiment in the group with new ways of behaving.

MONOPOLIZERS

In most groups, the role of the "monopolizer" emerges in which a person dominates the group discussion. "Letting the person continue on without containment is not good for group process, because other members may disengage or become frustrated with the overbearing, dominant group member. In addition, the group leaders may not be able to cover the items on the agenda for the group if too much time is taken up by one group member" (Bieling, 2006, p. 100).

Question 13.1: In your classes, have you noticed the emergence of a "monopolizer"? If so, how do your instructors handle this behavior? Does it seem effective? If you were leading the class, how would you handle the behavior? Write your answers here before reading on.

An initial strategy with monopolizing behavior is to redirect the group interactions: "Remember we have a rule about equal participation. Let's give someone else an opportunity to share and, if we have time, we can get back to you." Or, "There are quite a few people who are interested in sharing, some of whom we haven't heard from yet." Or, "We need to move on now because we have a lot of material to cover today." A compliment on the person's expertise, knowledge, and/or experience of a topic or the ability to articulate concerns can take the sting out of the redirection: "I know you have learned a lot about brain injury, John," or "You have been coming to group for a long time, so you know a lot about the topics we've been talking about."

An additional strategy is to ask the group member who is telling a long, detailed, and drawn-out story, the purpose of the story and how it relates to the discussion at hand or what is wanted from the group by telling this story. An alternative tactic is to ask the group members these same questions, which has the effect of helping them gain ownership of the group interactions and letting monopolizers know that a story may irrelevant, buried in detail, and so forth, and the group does not know how to help.

If the above approaches do not work, the group leader can engage the monopolizer in a discussion of the behavior (see above in overall strategy). The advantages and disadvantages of the behavior can be listed, drawing out the group member's insights and the perspectives of other participants. Potential advantages are: 1) to avoid self disclosure; 2) to entertain; 3) to gain attention; 4) to justify his or her position; 5) to present grievances; and 6) to control the group. The disadvantages are that the monopolizer is not trying out new behaviors in group and, therefore, is protecting him or herself from change. Additionally, this tactic prevents others from relating to the person. As Yalom (2005) notes, your goal, as the group leader, is not simply to silence monopolizers but to help them meaningfully engage and to see how their interaction pattern may play itself out in venues outside the group.

The monopolist may devalue the importance of learning about the group's reaction to her. Yalom suggests honest self-examination and group feedback for such clients to tap into the roots of their interpersonal difficulties. He writes,

> *What is different in the group is the presence of norms that permit the others to comment openly on [a member's] behavior. The therapist increases therapeutic leverage by encouraging the patient to examine and discuss interpersonal difficulties in their [sic] life; loneliness, lack of close friends, not being listened to by others, being shunned without reason...Once these are made explicit, the therapist can, more convincingly, demonstrate to monopolistic clients the importance and relevance of examining their in-group behavior (Yalom, 2005, p. 397).*

A final approach to managing monopolizers (especially in the presence of one or more members who do not speak), is to conduct the group in a "round robin" style. In this style of leadership, the group leader instructs the members to each share in turn for a certain amount of time, for example, approximately three minutes, so that every one gets an equal chance to participate in the group.

The following example is from a closed psychoeducational group for survivors of sexual assault. There are two facilitators, one is a graduate social work intern and the other is a volunteer.

Intern:	Before we get started, let's check in. How is everyone doing tonight?
Group member #1:	I'm a bit shaken up. I was in a car accident today.
Volunteer:	Wow... are you okay?
Group member #1:	Yeah, it wasn't major... but it shook me up.
Group member #2:	Hey, I know how you feel. I was in a car accident the other day—now my mom is driving me around.
Volunteer:	Wow—just not a good time for us and cars!
Group member #3:	I was arrested this weekend for driving while intoxicated! I had to spend the night in jail—I'm so ashamed! That's never happened to me before.

Group member #2:   My mom has been harping on me ever since I got in the accident. See, my mom and I don't have a good relationship. She doesn't quite understand where I'm coming from on things. She still thinks I wasn't sexually assaulted. But it's always been that way with her. My dad was the only one in my family that ever really cared about me —but we didn't have a good relationship until a few years before he died. My dad was schizophrenic, and he had anger problems, but he was on his medication and going to counseling—he'd worked through some of the stuff in his past... and a few years before he died we would talk, about all kinds of things. And so...

Intern: I hate to cut you off. I'm really glad that you feel comfortable sharing this with the group—and I do think it's important. But we need to start talking about the topic for tonight—and we want to make sure everyone has a chance to talk. Are you okay with us moving on?

Group member #2:   Oh yeah... I'm sorry.

Volunteer and intern: That's all right.

The following describes the intern's processing of this event:

> *Group member #2 often monopolizes the group's time, providing a lot of unnecessary background material when relating events. The volunteer and I had been discussing this ongoing problem in private. We did not want to alienate the group member or make her feel unaccepted in the group. But we also did not want the other members to feel hampered in being able to speak.*
>
> *Since I was group member #2's individual counselor, one option we had discussed was for me to bring the matter up privately with group member #2 in individual counseling. The benefit to this approach would be the avoidance of possibly embarrassing the member in front of the rest of the group. The possible downside to this method would be that the group member may feel too embarrassed to return to the group in fear that the other members felt the same way. It may come across to her that the matter is much bigger than we had intended.*
>
> *A further option was for us to reiterate the group rules of ensuring that all members have a chance to talk, and avoid pointing a finger at anyone in particular. This method, however, was determined to be too indirect. We attempted this in a previous group, but the group member was unable to see how her behaviors were making it difficult for the rest of the group members to share.*
>
> *The third method was to address the matter as it occurred within the context of the group by reiterating the purpose of the group and redirecting the conversation. This third method was chosen by us as the least shame inducing.*
>
> *We also decided that I would follow up with group member #2 in our next individual session after we addressed her behavior in group. I would ask her how she was feeling about the intervention in group as a way of facilitating conversation regarding the members' perceptions of her interaction patterns in the group.*

Question 13.2: Based on the group scenario and the student intern's thinking on the subject, what is your reaction of how this was handled? How might you have handled this situation differently?

The following scenario involves an open-ended, facilitator-led support group for adult survivors of brain injury and their families to "take charge of their recovery." The goal of the group was to share experiences, develop coping strategies, become more knowledgeable about medical information, and learn about community resources. The purpose of this particular meeting was to explore depression as related to brain injury.

Intern:	Many people with brain injury may experience depression. The research shows that anywhere from 30 to 49% have depression. Today, we're going to talk about your experiences with depression. What's your reaction to these statistics?
John:	That seems too small of a number. What I have experienced is not just depression, but frustration that becomes anger that becomes depression. And sometimes I just can't handle it because I get so tired.
Pam:	Me too, plus what worked to get rid of depression before the accident, doesn't work any more. So I'm left trying new things with what seems like half of the original equipment.
Intern:	That's a very good point! The brain regulates your moods and emotions, but with the brain injury, this system is altered and one must find new strategies to address all of the anger, frustration, and fatigue that comes with brain injury.
John:	I am so mad at the doctors, they think that they know everything and that they are "gods." Half of them don't know that changes in the brain because of an injury can make what we experience look like depression, but it's not depression.
Intern:	So what I hear you say is that brain injury and depression have a lot of things in common.
Pam:	I have had that experience when—
John:	*(interrupts)* Doctors are the problem! *(Louder voice)* They think that they know everything! They call everything that they don't understand depression. That makes me angry. *(pounds the table)*
Intern:	So you are trying to say is that it is a—
John:	They're dumb!
Intern:	So, you believe that they over diagnose depression?
John:	They diagnose by default because they don't want to take time out to really truly understand brain injury.
Pam:	You know. I had a bit of difficulty with my doctor when I first came in and said that I was sleepy a lot, my appetite changed, and I was not motivated—
John:	They're stupid doctors.

In this particular case, although there were 14 people present, most of the group's interactions revolved around John and, to a lesser degree, Pam. At this point, the group leader could invoke some of the group rules and follow some of the suggestions presented above. Moreover, people with brain injury may have less control over their reactions and anger, and a rule could acknowledge these limitations and mention that at times the group leader might need to signal to the group member who is possibly frightening other members to curb his or her behavior.

In a teen group on increasing coping skills, one girl, Kay, emerged as the monopolizer. She was always the first one to respond to a question or presentation of information; indeed the group members would wait for Kay to respond first and look to her. Kay would also tell long stories and repeat herself multiple times. Although she would listen when other group members spoke, she tended to direct the conversation back to what she was talking about. The group leaders attempted to curb her behavior by redirecting questions to the rest of the group when she paused or took a breath; however, they were unable to keep Kay in check for long.

Question 13.3: How would you handle this situation as a group leader?

The group modality of the prison substance-abuse treatment program has already been introduced. A student intern was once confused about how to handle a member who told incredibly long and fanciful stories about her past exploits, and she obviously enjoyed the attention she received from the other members. The intern had already asked the other group members about their reactions to the storyteller, and they all seemed to be enthralled with her entertaining stories. This left the student intern uncertain how to proceed, but many of the ideas on how to handle monopolizers can be used in this and similar situations.

Question 13.4: How would you handle a highly dramatic member, such as the one described here?

QUIET AND PASSIVE MEMBERS

As well as people who want to dominate the group, another characteristic pattern is for one or more members to be silent. "The important point is that silence is never silent; it is behavior and, like all other behavior in the group, has meaning both in the framework of the here-and-now and as a representative sample of the patient's typical way of relating to his interpersonal world" (Yalom, 2005, p. 386).

Question 13.5: What are the reasons that people are silent in group situations and what strategies would you use to handle these silent members?

There are various reasons why people are silent (Yalom, 2005):

- Anxiety and feelings of inadequacy
- Shyness and inhibition
- Cultural belief that it is inappropriate to talk a lot or self-disclose
- Uncertainity of group expectations of them
- Avoidance/distance keeping
- Fear of displaying weakness
- Afraid of loss of control should they become emotional or cry

Different writers on groups have come up with various ways to handle silent members (Corey et al., 2008; Toseland & Rivas, 2009):

- Ask, "We haven't heard from everyone today, and I wonder if someone we haven't heard from would like to add something at this point?" This technique means that no one in particular is singled out.

- Positively reinforce members who are normally quiet for their contributions and the value of their feedbacks or comments when they do take a risk and talk.

- Directly ask questions such as "What do you think about what so and so is saying?" or "You have some experience with this, what do you think?" This, however, has the disadvantage of singling out silent members, and they might feel "put on the spot."

- Inquire whether the silence is characteristic of their way of relating outside the group, and remind them that the group can be an opportunity to try out new behaviors.

- Use a round robin style in which each person has to respond to a particular question or certain material if there are a few quiet members and a monopolizer.

In the brain injury support group mentioned on page 153, Tomoko is the only Asian American member and new to the group. Tomoko can speak English, although her speech is heavily accented. She is attentive and participates non-verbally, although not verbally.

Question 13.6: Based on the limited information you have, what could be some of the reasons for her silence? How would you handle these possible reasons?

HELPERS

The "helper" habitually gives advice to others as the example of a support group for mothers in recovery shows:

Leader:	Who would like to start?
Client 1:	Well, I just reconnected with my kids this weekend for the first time in months. I mean I had them at my house. They was gettin' on my nerves. I just felt so overwhelmed. I was like "am I ready for this?" I'm just not sure I am ready to be back with them again.
Leader:	So you have been apart from your children and you are just starting to get used to them again?
Client 1:	Yeah. We had a sleepover. All four of them were there and we made popcorn and watched a movie. It was fun but they were also gettin' on my nerves. I was starting to feel overwhelmed.
Client 2:	You know Client 1, you're doing a good job. Having kids can be stressful for anyone but especially because you are just getting back with them and reestablishing your relationships. Plus, you are going through your own stuff, you know? You've been clean now for what, 60 days? That's tough, you know? But you just have to take it a day at a time. When I'm with my two kids I get stressed out. They work on me and get on my nerves. But I have to remember myself and my own needs too, you know?
Client 1 *(nods):*	Yes, I still focus on myself, too.

Client 3: I'm trying to get my daughter back. I don't have custody of her no more. She will be 18 soon though. I'm hoping I can get her back.

Leader: Let's focus on what Client 1—

Client 2: Client 3, you have a tough situation, you know? I don't know what its like to have custody taken from me but it must be very hard, you know? You have to remember that you have an illness though and your needs are important, too. I think if you just keep working on yourself and your own issues you will be able to get your daughter back. That's what I did in my situation. I just worked on myself, and I keep working on myself everyday and now things are getting easier with my kids.

Leader: Client 2, I would like to hear what Client 3 thinks—

Client 2: And if you just stay on task and keep focusing on yourself, that's the only way you will get your own issues resolved so that you can reunite with your daughter again. You know? Are you taking your medication, Client 4? You know it's important to keep taking your meds so you can keep your illness under control, right? If we don't all keep following with our own treatment, then we are going to keep having difficulty with our relationships with our kids.

Leader: I would like to go to Client 1 for a minute—

One of the main problems with this behavior is that the person tends to make broad generalizations about other people's experiences, which may or may not be accurate (Bieling et al., 2006). For instance, Client #2 talks about how other group members should concentrate on their own needs. Although the statement seems solicitous, it is really just prescribing general advice that may or may not be helpful for the group member. It lacks specificity. Even if we are to decide that "focusing on your own needs" is important, what does that mean for the group members? How are they not focusing on their needs right now? What will it take for them to focus on their needs? How will they balance their needs with the needs of their children? The sweeping generalizations Client #2 makes serve to keep the group on a superficial level and further exploration is blocked.

Note also how Client #2 seems to imply that she no longer has the problems that are bringing her to group as in the following statement: "I think if you just keep working on yourself and your own issues, you will be able to get your daughter back. That's what I did in my situation. I just worked on myself, and I keep working on myself everyday and now things are getting easier with my kids." By putting herself in the "helping" role, she does not permit herself to receive assistance from the group with the problems she is working on. It may seem that these members are problem free, and one might wonder why they even joined the group. It is important for these members to learn that the group is a source of help "...where they can learn to receive from others, and where they can decide whether their giving style is working for them or whether they might not profit from adding other dimensions to themselves" (Corey et al, 2008, p. 93).

Another problem with "helping" is that sometimes the advice contradicts the information provided in the group (Bieling et al., 2006). One common example takes place in treatment groups for anxiety disorders in which an important aim is to expose people to what they fear so that the anxiety eventually dissipates. In such groups, a helper might encourage other members to avoid anxiety-triggering situations. Bieling et al. (2006) make the following suggestion for handling this kind of advice.

In such a case, the group leader can take the advice back to the group by asking group members what they think about it, or how the suggestion fits with what they have learned in the group so far.

In this way the "unhelpful" or countertherapeutic suggestion is dealt with in a constructive manner that is processed in the group to enhance or reinforce the underlying principles or objectives of the therapeutic approach. The group leader could also ask the member who volunteered the suggestion what he or she thought the benefits or costs of taking the advice would be (e.g., reducing anxiety in the short term, but reinforcing it in the long term) (Bieling et al., 2006, p. 111).

What can the group leader do in other "helping" situations? One way to handle this type of behavior is to probe for more specificity. For example, the group leader can ask Client #1, "When you were talking about your children getting on your nerves and you were feeling so overwhelmed, what was going on?" This simple statement asks Client #1, after Client #2 has spoken very generally about her own and Client #1's situation, to be more concrete about her particular situation. By identifying what exactly was difficult for her about having her children in the home, she can clarify her thoughts and feelings about her experience and the work that needs to be done can proceed from there.

Let's say at that point the "helper" returned to her patterned behavior and inserted another variation about Client #1 having to take care of her own needs. The leader may then have to provide a rationale for why it is important to stay with Client #1's concerns. "In order to be helpful, we have to find out what is going on for Client #1, and she needs some time to explore what was challenging for her about being with her children. What thoughts was she having? What behaviors in her children did she find particularly difficult? How did she handle these? Go on, Client #1." If the "helper" still insists on continuing with the same pattern of behavior, then the group leader might process these interactions, using the overall strategy as provided above (see page 150).

DEVIL'S ADVOCATE/NAY-SAYER

A troublesome pattern in groups is when one person chronically demonstrates negativity in group, frequently questioning or challenging information that is presented. If this pattern becomes problematic, the group leader may have to ask the identified group member and the other participants to talk about its advantages and disadvantages. The positive aspects of this behavior can be congratulated, such as the person is engaging in critical thinking; is listening attentively; and is asking good questions. A main, but questionable advantage, is that nay-saying plays a protective role; that is, the person does not have to change or take risks and get hurt. However, there are many disadvantages: such people remain stuck in their behaviors; their behavior drains the energy of the group; their pattern often repulses others, and relationships may suffer as a result.

CLOWN

The clown role is not limited to children, although this pattern of behavior may be easier to see when children act out and get others to laugh at their antics. Clowns can emerge in adult groups; these are people who constantly rely on humor as a defense and as a way to interact with others. When asked the role they play in group, such people may or may not be able to identify themselves as clowns, but other group members certainly will. The advantages (helps one cope, others enjoy it, eases tension in social situations, protects one from possibly painful inner reflection) and the disadvantages (keeps other people from getting close, avoids deep feelings and authenticity in oneself and in others) may need to be explored.

SUMMARY

This chapter has revealed different role behaviors that emerge in groups that can potentially derail the group process. We have discussed a number of different strategies for approaching such behaviors, and will turn in the next chapter to other potential challenges group leaders may encounter.

Chapter 14
Challenges to Group Leadership

When you are the group leader, people might challenge your authority, question the purpose of the group or the curriculum, or why they have to attend. They may vent strong emotions, such as anger. The group leader strives to remain non-reactive and refrains from jumping to his/her own defense, even though this is a natural tendency. Note that we have already talked extensively about how to plan and implement groups so as to avoid problems. Further, we have discussed working with clients who have been mandated to attend groups. However, the nature of groups is that they are made up of a collection of unique individuals, who together create a distinctive group complexion. One cannot always predict what will emerge but this chapter will help you feel more prepared for some of the common challenges that groups bring:

- Handling personal questions
- Challenging Leader's Qualifications
- Being Seen as a Failure as a Group Leader
- Managing Psychotic Symptoms
- Lack of Participation
- Inappropriate Participation
- Disruptive Side Conversations
- Disagreement with the Leader
- Managing Conflict

HANDLING PERSONAL QUESTIONS

Often, group members ask leaders personal questions, putting them on the spot and causing discomfort. How could you handle the following types of situations?

- Group members ask if the leader has experienced the same problem as their own. If leaders do have the problem, do they say so? If they don't, they are often challenged by group members asserting that they won't be able to understand what the group members are going through.
- Group members ask personal questions (Have you ever used drugs? When did you first have sex?).

Question 14.1: How would you respond to each of these situations? Write your answer here before reading on.

It should be reassuring to learn that you don't have to divulge personal and intimate information in either of the above situations. You may find that the following choice of responses is often helpful:

- Reflect back what seems to be the underlying concern: "You're worried that if I don't share your problem, then I won't know enough to be able to help you." Or "You're worried that I may not have enough experience to be able to help you."
- If any of these questions are asked by those who have had previous group treatment experiences, put them in the expert role (also see strengths-based chapter) by asking them: "Tell me what has been helpful for you from group leaders in past group experiences; tell me what has not been so helpful, so I can make sure to avoid those things with you."
- "Tell me what I need to understand about your experience so I can help you."

If group members ask specific and personal questions of the group leader, such as "Do you have HIV? When did you first have sex?"):

- Invite exploration rather than reacting defensively, "Can you tell me your reasons for wanting to know?" and then respond to those reasons. Some of them may be related to the above, i.e., wanting to find out if the group leader has enough knowledge about the problem/experience.
- Make a statement such as the following: "Regardless of whether I have had an addiction (or experienced depression, been divorced, abused, or any other number of life situations that group members may explore), I can't possibly know what the experience has been like for you specifically unless I have walked in your shoes."
- Tune in to what the member is revealing with the question, including their own insecurities and doubts that can be addressed in the leader's response.

To start, ask, "I'm wondering how you think knowing this will be helpful to you?" Responses may vary as the following: "I want to know if you're as perfect as you seem," "if you've ever had any problems," or "we talk about ourselves, don't we get to hear about you?" The leader can then cater his or her response to what members reveal: "So problems mean we are imperfect?" which can open up how they feel about their "problem." Or, "We all have problems, and everyone's problem is unique and handled differently depending on what it is, but no one is immune from experiencing problems in his or her life." Or acknowledging that "it is difficult to reveal ourselves, especially when we don't know everything about the people we are talking to. Hopefully, enough trust will develop to share, and over time, it is likely that you will learn a little about me too."

Question 14.2: Consider the open-ended recovery support group found on pages 134-135. How do you think the group leader handled the challenge of responding to the group member's question whether she was in recovery? What other statements might you be comfortable making in such a situation?

Question 14.3: Recall the scenario of the teen process group in the residential treatment center (see page 22) when the leader was asked about her sexual experiences. What do you think about the way she handled the teens' questioning? What other ways could she have managed the situation?

CHALLENGING LEADER'S QUALIFICATIONS

A particular fear of youthful students and/or those with little experience is that their age and/or competence will be questioned. The question generally indicates the members' desperation about their plight and their doubts about whether anyone can help them. As a leader, you need not deny if you are young, nor assure your competence as that will be revealed over time. A simple statement, such as, "Let's see what we can all do together to make this a positive group experience" may help people see they are not alone with their problem, and that the first step is giving the group and the leader a chance.

Question 14.4: In a parenting group for welfare-to-work mothers, members with more parenting experience questioned the leaders' competence on the grounds that neither of the two had children. How would you handle such a challenge?

In a psychoeducational group in a partial hospitalization program, a member accused an undergraduate student intern of being unqualified to lead such a group. Rather than responding to this client in an angry fashion, the intern calmly assured the clients that although she was still attending classes, she was qualified to facilitate the group and that she did so under the supervision of the lead counselors of the program.

Question 14.5: What do you think of the intern's response? What other ways could she have handled this challenge?

Question 14.6: Refer again to the "Katie" group leader scenario (pages.23-24) when she took over the group. How do you think she handled the questioning of her credentials?

BEING SEEN AS A FAILURE AS A GROUP LEADER

A number of students have mentioned that one of their worst fears is to be told, "You're the worst group leader I've ever had." There are a couple of different options at this point for the group leader:

- Put the client in the expert position by finding out, "Tell me what has been helpful from group leaders in past group experiences; tell me what has not been so helpful, so I can make sure to avoid those things with you."

- What would you be doing and saying in group if you had the best group leader you've ever had?

A remark about being a "bad group leader" could follow a difficult exchange between member and leader, to which the leader will likely want to refer, "You say that after I challenged your commitment to recovery; it sounds like you were taken aback by that?" or whatever else preceded the comment, as it is likely not spontaneous. The leader can then explore what prompted the statement. After that, the leader may compliment the speaker: "I am glad you are able to express that to me, and I can hear there is disappointment," and can reflect the concern: "What do you think we can do to improve this situation to work together productively?" Note the use of the word "we" to emphasize that a relationship does exist and can be improved upon with work, just as can other relationships in the member's life.

MANAGING PSYCHOTIC SYMPTOMS

As discussed, active psychosis (delusions, hallucinations, disorganized speech, and so forth) are usually a rule out for group participation, unless, of course, the group is set up for people with severe mental illness. Students and social work professionals often serve clients who have psychotic disorders in various in-patient and out-patient settings, and Yalom (1985) states the advantages of groups for these populations. First, he claims that many times presenting symptoms, especially when a person has been hospitalized, are due to decompensation from a real or threatened loss of an important relationship. Additionally, many people with severe mental illness display "...chronic interpersonal problems—for example, isolation and loneliness, poor social skills, sexual concerns, conflicts around authority, anger, intimacy, and dependency...[and] the group is the therapeutic arena par excellence in which patients learn to explore and to correct maladaptive interpersonal patterns" (Yalom, 1985, p. 33). For such clients the group offers support, structure, a way to orient to the environment, helps focus members' attention, and improves socialization with the staff and other program attendees.

Certain challenges are involved, however, in leading groups with people with severe mental illness. Sometimes remarks made by such group members can be unrelated to the topic at hand because of delusions, hallucinations, or disorganized speech. Several options are available based on the nature of what is said. For instance, if a thread of the conversation exists, you can redirect the comment. In the health education group held for those with severe mental illness in a residential treatment facility, one of the members, Alex says, "I'm not going to let them give me AIDS. You can't make me take my medicine. I'll have you arrested. I had Cindy and that guy with a beard arrested. They are in jail for five years. Diabetes isn't real. Five hundred is a normal blood sugar. I'll bet your blood sugar is 500." The student intern could then redirect the comment to the group as a whole by asking, "What is a normal blood sugar, do you know?" In general, the group leader avoids countering such statements or reinforcing them and instead says, "John, this group is about _____. I don't want to go too far from our topic." In this way, group leaders can encourage reality-based conversations without demeaning or arguing the reality of members' thoughts.

Social Work Intern:	Alex, you have diabetes, can you tell us about your diet?
(Alex mutters something unintelligible.)	
Social Work Intern:	Sally, what about you? How do you control your diabetes?
Sally:	Um, I don't know. I eat sugar-free candy.
Social Work Intern:	That's one good way of managing your diabetes.
Alex *(breaks into conversation in a loud voice):*	My medication is poison. The CIA is trying to poison me. They are responsible for AIDS, which they made in a laboratory. First they infected all the faggots. Now they want to infect me with the needles. I know all about this...that's why they locked me up. I'm leaving here soon. I have a big house. *(Becomes even louder).* They're trying to kill me! I know all about it. The government is out to get me. They want me dead!

Question 14.7: From the health education group presented above, how would you handle Alex's remarks?

LACK OF PARTICIPATION

Group leaders often tell me they dread a lack of participation—long silences that they feel compelled to fill and lack of responses to the questions they or other group members pose. However, they also do not like when group members fail to take the group seriously and participate in a way that conveys this.

First, we will tackle lack of participation in groups:

1. Create group guidelines and expectations around participation (see Chapter 4).

For example, in a group for adolescent girls in the school setting, members treated the group leaders as they would their teachers, behaving as they would be expected to in a classroom. They waited to be addressed before speaking and would direct their comments to the leaders rather than the group. When the group topics became more sensitive and less school-related, members would look at the leaders apprehensively as though they expected them to censor the group members' comments. The members seemed to reject leader efforts to use group-centered leadership. For example, questions such as, "What do you all think about...?" received no response. Nor would the girls respond to each other spontaneously. They waited to be "called on" directly by the group leaders.

To prevent this norm from developing at the outset, the group leaders could have had a discussion in the first session about the differences between the way the group and the classroom were run, pointing out that the group was more informal. Members did not have to raise hands, get permission to speak, and could talk about topics that they might not address in school, such as handling sexual pressure. Further there were no "right" or "wrong" answers and rather than learning material, they were asked to self-disclose about more personal matters.

- Structure groups with behavioral reinforcement systems so that appropriate participation is rewarded (see Chapter 12).

- Use a "round robin" interaction style so that each group member is required to participate in turn.

- Allow silence so that group members understand that you will not give up or rescue them if they do not answer questions or initiate a conversation. Most of the time group members become sufficiently uncomfortable with the silence to start talking.

- Structure the groups with activities that demand participation.

The following excerpt also stems from the health education group at the residential facility for individuals with severe mental illness. In this situation, the group leader was concerned about the long silences between the times he spoke.

SW Intern: Today we've been talking about calories. Let's review what we discussed. Can someone tell me what an empty calorie is?

Mary: It's sodas, pie, ice cream, candy and that sort of thing...like Snickers, M&Ms, Butterfingers, cookies, pies, Mars, Coke, Root Beer, ice cream, chocolate, hard candy, Ginger Ale, Pepsi, Mountain Dew...

Tom: It's sugar. I don't eat a lot of sugar.

(A period of silence ensues.)

SW Intern: Thank you. Let's discuss what you all had for lunch today. Were there any empty calorie dishes served?

Henry: We had cake.

Tom: I didn't eat the cake. I ate the chicken and vegetables. Was that good?

SW Intern: Yes Tom, those were healthy choices. Cake is definitely a source of empty calories. What are some of the health concerns associated with empty calories?

Mary: They cause weight gain and diabetes...weight gain and diabetes. When I was at Western State I knew this lady who had diabetes because she drank a lot of sodas. She drank six sodas a day...six sodas a day. She had to take a shot everyday.

(More silence.)

SW Intern: That's a good point Mary. Does anyone else have anything to add?

Tom: I don't have diabetes. I work out. I'm not overweight. Am I in good shape?

SW Intern: Yes, Tom, it's good that you take care of yourself by exercising.

(More silence.)

In this situation, the intern could search for a health education curriculum designed for people with severe mental illness that was activity-based. If group members engaged in activities, such as choosing pictures of balanced meals from several selections, they would then be able to share the results of what they did with the group. Talking about an activity one performs is sometimes less threatening than responding to open-ended questions, although the student intern in this situation did a nice job of posing questions to engage the group members in discussion.

2. Hold a conversation about the norms that have developed in group around lack of participation.

Say, for example, in the adolescent girls' group in the school setting, that the group members received initial orientation as to the rules and guidelines; yet the situation as described above developed. In this case, the group leaders could ask the group members to reflect on their level of participation in the group and share their observations. If necessary, they could ask how safety could be increased in group so that the girls would feel comfortable taking more risks.

A particular type of lack of participation involves "I don't know" responses. Children and adolescents who are mandated to treatment may tend to respond with "I don't know" when asked questions in a group. This response can be frustrating for group leaders, but there are a variety of strategies to use in this situation:

1. Allow silence (about 20-30 seconds).
2. Rephrase the question.
3. Ask a relationship question (see page 100).
4. Say, "I know you don't know, so just make it up," which bypasses the resistance or the fear that a group member doesn't know or doesn't have the right answer.
5. Redirect the question to the entire group.

Question 14.8: Refer again to the adolescent sex-offender group presented on pages 63-64. For each of the "I don't know" responses made by Group member 1, talk about what strategies you would use in order to move him into making more appropriate responses.

INAPPROPRIATE PARTICIPATION

Inappropriate participation will be defined here as participation that does not relate to the purpose of the group, and comments that are disrespectful to other participants and/or group leaders. Many of the strategies discussed in the last section (creating group guidelines and expectations around appropriate participation, structuring the group sessions with activities, using a behavioral reinforcement system) have relevance here. Recall also that the initial planning of groups has much to do with their later success. Is there a clearly defined purpose to the group that serves the population who is receiving services? Is there a relevant and empirically validated curriculum in place? How have group members been oriented to the group? Finally, when group members do not take the group seriously, they have often been mandated to attend group services; therefore, you can draw on many of the techniques discussed in Chapter 9.

Two student interns facilitated an educational group for adolescents in the foster care Independent Living Program. The focus of this particular session was to discuss the use of self-defense and "staying safe." The group consisted of three parts: a verbal quiz on street smarts, a group discussion concerning street smarts and self-defense, and an interactive self-defense workshop with a detective from the local county. An excerpt will follow:

Student intern #1:	So can you think of things you can do to stay safe?

(Silence.)

J:	Remember whoever contributes gets a piece of candy!
T:	I know! You should carry a knife!
Student intern #1:	Do you think that would be a safe thing to do or would carrying a knife possibly make a situation more dangerous?
N:	*(interrupting)* I have a question about that—what if a knife is over five inches? Can you have it at your foster home?
Student intern #2:	I think that would be a great question for the detective when she comes in, but for now can anyone think of ways to stay safe? For example what should you do if you're walking down the street and notice that someone is following you?
B:	Stop and act like you're crazy. No one will mess with you if they think you're crazy.

Question 14.9: In this situation, the interns were worried about the way the group members did not seem to take the group seriously. They also were uncomfortable about the way the group members yelled out their responses. What measures would you take to rectify the situation if you were the group leader?

DISRUPTIVE SIDE CONVERSATIONS

Dyads have their advantages, for instance, having a personal relationship with at least one other person in the group may lead a person to feel more connected to the group. Sometimes, however, dyads can become unhelpful, in terms of "cliques" that wield negative power in the group and exclude others. They also may foster "side conversations," which can become disruptive to the group.

The initial strategy is to promote the development of norms that emphasize one person talking at a time and the importance of listening and respecting other group members (Toseland & Rivas, 2009). If side conversations become a problem, one strategy is to change seating arrangements and to rotate dyads as activities are presented to the group. I implement this strategy in the classroom for small group activities; otherwise, the same people, usually those who sit next to each other and who already know each other, will always participate in group activities together. As a result of rotating dyads, all class members get to know each other in the service of group cohesiveness.

"Talking sticks," in which only the person holding the stick can speak, can also be used when children have difficulty allowing one person to talk at a time. When the group members get used to giving one person "the floor," the stick can eventually be phased out.

DISAGREEMENT WITH THE LEADER

One type of situation that leaders generally dread is if a group member disagrees with them or criticizes the material that is being presented. One of the main advantages of group intervention is that the leader can avoid power struggles and redirect critical comments to the whole group. Other members can typically confront a fellow group member with more credibility than can a group leader because of the increased identification among peers.

The following excerpt is from a dialectical behavior therapy for people with a diagnosis of borderline personality disorder.

Group Leader: It is important to be in touch with our emotions, to understand what we are feeling and why, but not to let them control us. The goal is to be aware of our emotions, but distant enough from them that we are not acting out from that emotional state.

Barbara: I don't have a problem with that. I didn't even need to do the homework. There are so many times when people just piss me off, but then I think "it's a beautiful day, I'm almost off work. I can smoke a cigarette real soon. I don't want to let this person set me off and ruin my day." So I ignore them and do my job. Then I just ride away on my bicycle.

Group Leader: Sounds like you're using the logical mind, and you're not letting the emotional mind take over when you get upset. That's what you should do; sounds like you're doing it well. But the question is, do you let yourself feel what you're feeling?

Barbara: There's no point. I just want to get away from them. I've come to the conclusion that people suck. There are people that really, really irritate me, and I don't want to deal with them. I just get on my bicycle and pedal along and enjoy the day. Then I go home to my kitty-cat.

Group Leader: You're right, some people are really irritating and hard to deal with. And that's great that you don't get into an altercation with those people. But I'm wondering what happens when you don't process your feelings about negative interactions with people. Are you finding it difficult to deal with times when you can't just ride away?

Barbara: It's like I said. I have a hard time with some people, and I just would rather not interact with them at all. I tell myself to just get through the day, and then I can leave it all behind me.

In this situation, the group leader was the individual therapist of this particular client and knew that the client had difficult interactions with others at times that caused problems for her at work. What are options for the group leader at this point since she has seemingly reached an impasse with this particular group member?

The group leader could redirect a general comment to the entire group, such as, "What are your reactions to what Barbara is saying?" or ask a more specific question, such as "When do you decide to just blow off something and when do you decide to do something about it?" [Answer: When a person has an ongoing relationship with the other person.] Since dialectical behavior therapy is a cognitive-behavioral package of intervention, the group leader could also ask the group members whether they could detect the presence of all-or-nothing thinking in Barbara's statements.

Question 14.10: Recall the topic *Substitute the Thoughts (page 149)*. Is there any example here of unrealistic thinking? If so, how could it be addressed in the group?

A general tip for leaders is that when people make characterological references to the leader ("you don't care," "you act like you know everything"), you can remain calm and ask for specific behaviors: "What is it I do that makes you think that?" This is an opportunity to model getting feedback in a non-defensive way. The most important thing for the group leader is to listen "...and avoid reacting too quickly and in a defensive manner" (Corey et al, 2008, p. 109).

Some criticisms of the group leader might serve to deepen the relationship of a group member to the group and to the group leader. For instance, an intern co-leader describes the following transaction in a "Girl Power!" group implemented in the school and designed to reduce risk and build resilience in 10-year-old girls to prevent future substance use. During one group, the girls were making chocolate chip cookies. Every girl was supposed to do a part of the recipe. There, however, were not enough to go around so the intern had two girls add the sugar. One of the girls got particularly upset and said, "I never get to do anything special in the group and that no matter what I do, no one ever pays attention to me, especially [the intern]." The intern was surprised at her reaction but acknowledged her concern and asked for input for ways in which the group and the intern could work at being better able to meet her needs. Some of the other girls in group responded with empathy and came up with ways to address this particular girl's concern. Specifically, one of the other girls traded "parts" with her, and this particular girl was able to pour the chocolate chips into the cookie mix. She seemed pleased with the response from the group and realized the importance of sharing her feelings and acknowledging her own needs by making a direct request. This example demonstrates that criticism of the leader was an attempt by a group member to become more vulnerable and to self-disclose more deeply about feeling left out and not treated specially. This became a "healing moment" as she learned that the risk lead to acceptance. This type of exchange may be more characteristic of the middle stage of group development. (See Chapter 7.)

MANAGING CONFLICT

Leaders often find the prospect of conflict in groups extremely uncomfortable. In Chapter 4, we talked about laying out to members the guidelines for group behavior; that process will set some beginning norms about respectful behavior to others. In Chapter 6, we talked about how to help members personalize reactions to others in group and offer appropriate feedback. This latter guideline for group behavior will typically forestall potential conflict from erupting. We have also discussed in Chapter 12 handling conflict through communication skills. An advantage of groups is that when conflict seems to escalate between two people, the other group members can be called upon to note their reactions and/or offer input. As a general guideline, we will distinguish between ways to manage conflict when it occurs in an open-ended group format that has remained in the beginning stage of group and when it occurs in a closed-ended group in which members have come to know each other over time.

A good example of conflict occurring in an open-ended group is the quarrel that erupted between the two women over "super-dependence." The group leader could stop the interaction pattern ("Let me stop you right there") and call upon the rest of the group members ("Let's hear about other people's reactions to this topic"). In order to structure the discussion, she could write "relying upon others"[1] on a poster-board sheet and ask the other group members, what do you see as the "good things" and the "not so good things" about relying on others. In an open-ended group eternally caught up in the beginning stages of group, a structured reaction by the group leader will provide a safe forum for further discussion and will hopefully defuse the conflict between the two members.

In a closed-ended group, conflict often signals that the group is entering the middle stage of group (see Chapter 7). The leader's responsibility in these situations is to model effective communication when conflict arises rather than ignoring or hiding from the conflict. Denying conflict is likely to give the message that conflict is negative and painful. Leaders might also find it helpful to reframe conflict among group members (for both themselves and for members) as a sign that the group is going to a deeper place and is capable of valuable work. Here are other ways to reframe conflict in the group as a positive experience:

1. Remind group members that people who have conflicts with each other can stimulate growth in the other.
2. Sometimes conflict can demonstrate that one cares deeply enough about the other person to feel anger.
3. Conflict can bring issues to awareness and is a way of learning about ourselves and our interactive patterns, and members who challenge us to see things differently can facilitate this process.
4. Conflict may arise because people sometimes see negative aspects of themselves in other people. One way, therefore, to deflect conflict, is to ask people what bothers them about the way the other person interacts. The leader can then inquire whether these attributes are anything with which the person can identify or has heard before about him or herself.

[1]The term "relying on others" seems to be a better use of language than "super-dependence" because it does not set up an extreme dichotomy and takes it account a more realistic appraisal of the risks and benefits involved in trusting others.

5. Since "envy is often an integral part of interpersonal conflict, it is often constructive to ask adversaries to talk about those aspects of one another that they admire or envy" (Yalom, 2005, p. 470). Members can become jealous, or resentful, of what other members appear to have or what they want and do not have, and will at times minimize or dispute the accomplishments or gains of others, thus creating conflict.

For example in the addiction recovery process group in the halfway house setting, when Jim announces to the group that he obtained employment and shares the personal benefits he gets from working, Alan, who has been unsuccessfully looking for work, responds as follows:

When Alan is able to acknowledge this, the leader can pursue with Alan and the rest of the group, "What do you think Jim has done to allow him to achieve his goal?" In this way, Alan can identify what has been successful for others in reaching their goals, and start to identify the aspects of the other person that he admires or would like to emulate.

Alan: Is that minimum wage? There are a million jobs like that around. We could all work there if we wanted.

Jim:. I don't see you doing anything but sitting around doing nothing. At least I'm doing something

Leader: What is it like for you Alan, to hear that Jim found work while it has been difficult for you?

Alan: As I said, anyone could work where he is;, I could get a job there any day.

Leader: But I asked what it is like for you to hear him talk about having a job, when you have been looking and not found one.

(This statement was made to bring Alan back to identifying the feeling that prompted his negative responses.)

Alan: I guess it's frustrating that he got a job so easily, but it's not a job I want anyway.

(Note how Alan acknowledges the frustration, but then downplays the job once again.)

Leader: What are you really frustrated with?

Alan: This whole thing—being unemployed, not working, other people getting on my case.

Leader: So it sounds like you would like to experience what Jim is talking about getting from working—the internal benefits—and how good he feels about it. Those are things you have also hoped for.

At times in groups, there may be situations when conflict appears to be gaining momentum and the leader is having difficulty managing it. In these situations, it may be helpful for the leader to simply say: "Let's stop right here," and to direct to the group: "What is going on here?", "What has happened?", or "Where did this get out of hand, and how can we bring it back to a more manageable place?" Sometimes people not directly involved with the client or clients engaged in conflict will say, "This doesn't involve me, so I don't want to be a part of it." To this, the leader can respond in such a way that will acknowledge the group as a unit: "We are all in this group together so we are all affected by this conflict and can participate in—and gain from—understanding it."

SUMMARY

The purpose of this chapter has been to cover particular challenges that may arise in group situations. Some of the commonalities in response to difficult situations are to react non-defensively, involve the group members in further discussion, and help them take responsibility for their recovery and the functioning of the group. By discussing how these challenges can be handled and having you think about and practice these skills, you will feel more prepared to meet these situations if they should occur.

Chapter 15
Groups and Social Diversity

Social workers can expect to lead groups in which people from different oppressed and vulnerable populations will participate, reflecting the traditional commitment of our field and the increasing diversification of society. You have likely learned through your masters in social work curriculum the importance of learning to work with people from diverse groups. These will include individuals from low socioeconomic status; minority ethnic and racial groups; immigrants; people with disabilities, including mental illness; gay, lesbian, bisexual, and transgendered individuals; women; and the elderly. Foremost, we want to follow the NASW Code of Ethics in treating each person with dignity and respect, and we will discuss in this chapter some other guiding principles and perspectives for working with diversity in groups. Although we will not be able to cover all socially diverse groups given our focus on group facilitation, selected examples will be chosen to illustrate key points.

KNOWLEDGE BASE

Under Cultural Competence and Social Diversity, the Code of Ethics (NASW, 1999) speaks to the need for social workers to possess a knowledge base of their clients' social diversity. By learning about people's beliefs, practices, experiences, and communities we may be able to understand and help people within their unique context. A couple of examples will be presented here to understand how this may operate in group interventions.

For instance, an intern who co-facilitated a group for men with HIV expressed astonishment at the number in the group of men who presented with either a current or past addiction problem. She became more accepting of the group participants' struggles when she understood the reasons that gay men and lesbians may be at risk for substance use problems (Beatty, Geckle, Huggins et al., 1999). First, gay bars, where alcohol is a main feature, is still one of the few legitimate places in most cities for meeting and socializing. Second, gays and lesbians are unable to fully partake in societal institutions that tend to attenuate substance use among heterosexuals, such as marriage and family life. Third, many gay and lesbian people do not have the full array of support from family, friends, and acquaintances. Loss of peers and acquaintances in the gay network is another burden to which the gay community is susceptible, which might lead to alcohol and drug use for coping with grief. Fourth, "(s)exual minority status may entail personal confrontation with prejudicial attitudes, discriminatory behaviors, unfairness and unequal power, hatred, and verbal, emotional, or physical abuse" (Beatty et al., 1999, pp. 545-546). The stress from discrimination may lead some people to cope through the use of alcohol or drugs. Along with the other risks substances pose, for gay males substance use might lower inhibitions and safe sexual practices, which, in turn, might lead to the possibility of HIV infection.

As another example of learning about the population with which one works, an intern co-leading a support group for African-American survivors of Hurricane Katrina said group members sounded "paranoid" when they blamed a government conspiracy for the flooding of their neighborhoods. When the intern learned through reading Henkel, Dovidio, and Gaertner (2006) that the government had flooded these areas in the past, it became clear to her why the group participants viewed events as they did.

In these examples, the group interns had a much different perspective on people's behavior once they learned more about their particular experiences and circumstances. These examples also show the necessity for group practitioners to develop awareness of their personal biases toward cultural groups. In this chapter, culture is defined to reflect, most broadly, the values, experiences, attitudes, and behaviors that a group of people might share. Therefore, it is not limited to just an ethnic heritage, but can mean "groups identified by age, gender, sexual orientation, religion, or socioeconomic status" (Corey & Corey, 2006, p. 16).

Question 15.1: In your group work with clients, identify some challenges you have experienced working with particular populations. What information was important for you to know about that particular group in order to understand their circumstances, perspectives, and responses to life situations? How did this change the way you reacted in the group situation? If you are currently being challenged, how can you find out information that will help you?

FINDING STRENGTHS

Although gaining knowledge about a particular group's history, customs, strengths, and struggles is encouraged, there exists no formulaic way to understand culture. Further, as DeJong and Berg (2002) state, "Each individual is a composite of several dimensions of diversity (class, ethnicity, gender, physical ability/disability, sexual orientation, race, religion, and so forth)" (p. 257). Therefore, group facilitators may have knowledge of and experience with a particular population, but they do not know a particular individual with a unique history, traits, strengths, and limitations. To make assumptions about that person because of cultural membership is tantamount to stereotyping. Instead, facilitators can respectfully inquire about members' worldview and their distinctive ways of approaching life's challenges (DeJong, Berg, Kleiner, & Mamiya, 2008). In line with this perspective, the NASW Code of Ethics cites that social workers should be aware of the strengths that exist in different cultures.

Other realities of current practice in group work affect the group worker's knowledge of how to work with certain populations. One is that in certain areas of the country, demographics and patterns of immigration are changing at a rapid pace; consequently, it is difficult to have knowledge of each cultural group with which one may interact. Another reality is that a facilitator may work with people from many diverse groups within a single intervention group. Although there may be common elements between ethnic minority cultures, such as the importance of family and spirituality, and the experience of discrimination, others may be different, such as patterns of immigration and acculturation (Muñoz & Mendelson, 2005).

Question 15.2: When has your knowledge about a certain cultural group fit particular clients, and when has it not, especially in a group intervention context?

For the many reasons listed above, the group facilitator can take a strengths-based view when working with people from diverse cultures. See Box 15.1 on page 178 for the types of questions that can be asked with ethnic minority clients as an example.

These lines of inquiry offer particular benefits for group social work. They draw out the cultural strengths of people, consistent with the NASW code mandate, without imposing prior knowledge of a particular group or stereotyping. These questions are also appropriate in groups comprised of culturally diverse members, so that the group leader can cultivate an awareness and explicit acknowledgement of similarities and differences between participants (Muñoz & Mendelson, 2005).

Question 15.3: The strengths-based questions listed in Box 15.1 are applied to ethnic minority populations. Can you come up with similar types of questions for other socially diverse populations with whom you work in group settings?

Box 15.1: Strengths-Based Questions for Working with Ethnic Minority Group Members

Culture	• What are the values in your culture that you take pride in? • Who are the role models in your community? Why? • How do you instill cultural knowledge and pride in your children? • What places in your community help foster a sense of community and positive identity?
Family and Relationships Many ethnic groups prize family and kinship ties and the value of interdependence (rather than the Western value of independence)	• Who are the most important people in your life? What do you most appreciate about _____? • What would they say are your best qualities as a _____ (spouse, parent, child, grandparent, etc.)? • What family rituals do you most enjoy? • Which relationships have been more challenging for you? How have you dealt with those challenges? • Whom can you go to for help? • Who has made a positive difference in your life? How so?
Parenting In some cultures, having children is one of people's most important life roles.	• What have you been willing to do for your children that you might not have done for yourself? • What would your children say about you that makes you a good parent? • When do you think you are able to be your best as a parent? • When do you most enjoy your children? What are you doing then? • How do you deal with parenting challenges? What qualities, behaviors, beliefs, and supports have you draw on? What qualities, behaviors, beliefs, and supports have developed as a result? • Who helps you be a good parent? • How can you take care of yourself so that you can be a good parent to your children? • What hopes do you have for your children? How do you want things to be different for them than they have been for you?
Spirituality and Religion Many people in ethnic minority cultures find spirituality and religion a source of meaning, coping, and solace.	• What are your spiritual beliefs that help you? • Do you attend a religious institution? How is this helpful for you? • What spiritual practices do you follow? How do these help?

USING THE EMPIRICAL LITERATURE AS A GUIDE

A theme of this workbook has been about finding curriculums that have already been tested with certain populations and problems. Unfortunately, empirically based guidance on how best to intervene with clients of diverse backgrounds, such as people of ethnic minorities, people with disabilities, females, and lesbian, gay, bisexual, and transgender individuals, is lacking (Brown, 2006; Levant & Silverstein, 2006; Olkin & Taliaferro, 2006; Sue & Zane, 2006). Discussion in the literature has centered on whether empirically based interventions can be applied to members of diverse groups and still maintain their effectiveness (Sue & Zane, 2006). In a unique analysis of this issue, Wilson, Lipsey, & Soydan (2003) examined interventions for teens in the juvenile justice system (many of these were carried out in a group format) and found they were equally effective for both Caucasian and African-American youth.

Another question in the literature is whether interventions that have been supported for mainstream groups can be altered to make them relevant for diverse groups; will they still maintain their effectiveness? (Sue & Zane, 2006). Some argue that with a sufficient level of clinical expertise, a facilitator can appropriately adapt an empirically based intervention to ensure that it is culturally sensitive. On the other side of the argument, slight adaptations may alter the treatment in important ways. In the next section, we will explore some ways to adapt curriculums to make them more germane for certain cultural groups.

Question 15.4: For a population with which you are working, do a search of the empirical literature to locate the group interventions that have been tested. Start, as described in Chapter 2 with the systematic reviews and meta-analyses that have been conducted, and work your way down from there.

CULTURALLY SENSITIVE ADAPTATIONS

Because most curricula have not been tested on socially diverse groups, facilitators may need to adapt them to accommodate the cultural beliefs, attitudes, and behaviors of the participants (Whaley & Davis, 2007). This may occur through delivery of services, changing the nature of the therapeutic relationship, and altering the components of the intervention. *Delivery of services* may involve the following:

- Offering a group in the language of the participants
- Having a member from the same culture as the participants lead the group
- Providing child care and transportation to clients who are impoverished
- Offering group services outside of mental health clinics.

Many people will avoid seeking mental health treatment due to stigma, suspicion, and financial reasons (U.S. Department of Health and Human Services, 2001). More acceptable venues for group services may involve settings, such as hospitals, health clinics, schools, and other community organizations (e.g., church) (Muñoz & Mendelson, 2005).

As an example of *changing the nature of the therapeutic relationship*, Miranda et al. (2007) describe that when recruiting minority women for a treatment outcome study on depression, many of the women did not recognize that their feelings and experiences were indicative of a treatable clinical disorder. Because of these women's lack of awareness of "depression," the researchers added an informational component in which the practitioner acted as "educator." In this way, the women could first learn about the problem of depression and how it could be treated. By attending the sessions, the women also built up a level of trust with the practitioner before entering treatment.

Altering the components of treatment may involve first, using culturally relevant language, explanations, and examples. For instance, in an adaptation of cognitive-behavioral group treatment for Latinos, Muñoz and Mendelson (2005) used "the saying *la gota de agua labra la piedra* [a drop of water carves a rock] to illustrate how thoughts, though transient, can gradually influence one's view of life and cause and maintain depression" (p. 792).

Altering components of treatment may also mean making didactic adaptations to the material. For instance, Kohn et al. (2002) modified the Muñoz (1984) curriculum for low-income African-American women with health problems and depression with the following content: 1) creating healthy relationships, which includes combating social isolation and deconstructing the Black Superwoman myth; 2) spirituality, which includes exploration of faith-based coping strategies; 3) the African-American family, which includes exploring inter-generational patterns of behavior and identifying strengths; and 4) African American female identity, which includes exploring and combating negative stereotypes and affirming strengths.

Another example of changing the presentation of material involves a support group for domestic violence victims, some of whom were immigrant women. When discussing the "power and control wheel," an educational tool that covers tactics used by abusive partners, the facilitator handed out a cultural adaptation that shows how women may be abused or controlled based on their immigrant status, such as threats to report her to immigration, to destroy her passport, or to take the children out of the country (Family Violence Prevention Fund, 2008).

Incorporating cultural values into the group intervention is another way to change service components. For instance, considering the importance of *familism* and *collectivism*, Muñoz and Mendelson (2005) discussed that many Latino immigrant clients are in the United States without family members, who remain in their countries of origin. As a result, intervention may address how to increase support networks, as well as keeping ties with family members who are at a distance.

Another important aspect of working with immigrant clients is to encourage a safe atmosphere for discussion of adaptation to the mainstream culture and the process of acculturation (Muñoz & Mendelson, 2005). Moreover, group leaders can promote exploration of group members' experiences of racism, prejudice, and discrimination, which can have a detrimental effect on a person's social and psychological functioning (Mickelson, 1999). Additionally, negative stereotypes can be internalized, which can damage an individual's sense of self-worth and adversely affect mental health (U.S. Department of Health and Human Services, 2001). Empowering strategies in groups include helping members challenge stereotypic beliefs, advising them of their rights and the resources available to them, and helping them become advocates for themselves, in line with the NASW ethic to promote social justice.

The following excerpt involves the "Relationship Skills" group that took place at a day treatment program for people with chronic mental illness (see pages 79-80). Group members (two of whom are African-American and three are Caucasian) complete a worksheet identifying problematic relationship behaviors. The group leader, a social work intern, is a young, Caucasian woman.

Recall that the conversation between two group members about "dependency in relationships" escalates into a conflict between the two. At one point, client #1 says, "You white girls have no idea what it is like to be a black woman in this city. You just have no idea." The fact that she made this statement seemed to indicate her experience was not being acknowledged; she appeared to feel misunderstood by at least the other group member, if not the group as a whole. Therefore, her statement could have deserved further attention.

Question 15.5: In this instance, how would you, as the group leader, say to get a discussion going in the group about this topic?

Read the following scenario, while considering how you would address this situation of internalized racism when it came up in an "empowering girls" group for four girls, ages nine and ten? Write your answer in the space provided. The social work intern and two of the group members are Caucasian. Carla, another group member, is African-American, and Bianca is Latina.

SW Intern:	Okay, now I'm a magic wizard and I'm going...
Bianca:	What's a wizard?
SW Intern:	It's someone with a magic wand. Okay, I'm waving my magic wand, and I'm going to turn....
Carla:	Would you please make me white? Please!!!!!!! Please!!!!!!
SW Intern:	*(in warm, calm voice)* Even if I could, I wouldn't think of changing anything about you. Why do you want to be white?
Carla:	Because I'm so ugly!
SW Intern:	You are certainly not ugly! You are absolutely beautiful; believe me.
Carla:	No, I'm not. I'm ugly!
SW Intern:	It seems to me that you have been telling yourself something that isn't true. I think you're beautiful. How about if we ask the other girls here what they think?
Carla:	Okay.

SW Intern: Jessie, would you please tell Carla what you think about her?

Jessie: I think she's really beautiful and I like her hair too.

Melissa: I think she's really pretty and beautiful. And she's nice too. And I like her blouse.

Bianca: I think you are sooooooooooooooooooo beautiful! I like your hair and blouse too. And your shoes.

SW Intern: Carla, did you hear what everyone said to you?

Carla: Yes, but I don't know.

SW Intern: Well, you have five people who all see you as beautiful. And there's one little voice in your head telling you you're ugly. So what you have to do now is set that little voice straight because it's wrong. However the idea that you're ugly got into your head, I don't know, but you can learn to not listen to it and eventually it will go away all together. So I've got homework for you. I want you to tell yourself 10 times a day "I am beautiful." Okay?

Carla: Okay.

SW Intern: Promise?

Carla: Promise. I think Jessie is really beautiful and so is Melissa and so is Bianca!

(Girls continue to exchange compliments.)

Question 15.6: What do you think of the way the student intern approached the situation? What did she do well? What didn't go as well?

Day treatment programs for people with severe mental illness often rely heavily on group services. One such program was located in a poor urban area in which only African-Americans lived. The stated theory of the agency was psychodynamic, and the goal of group intervention was to help the members process their early childhood experiences.

Question: 15.7: Part I. What do you think of using this theoretical framework with this population and problem area? Part II. Read Miranda et al. (2005) and conduct a literature review from 2005 to the present on interventions that might be effective in this setting with this population. What does the literature advise in terms of the appropriate intervention?

PUTTING IT ALL TOGETHER

These final questions will ask you apply the information provided in this chapter to your own experience working with diversity in groups. They also ask you to pull together the material, taking the different approaches discussed, to weave together acceptable responses when facilitating a group with socially diverse participants.

Question 15.8: What diverse groups do you work with in your field or social work employment setting? What challenges have arisen as a result of your work with these diverse groups? How are the services adapted to the needs of the population in terms of delivery, therapeutic process and relationship, and alterations in the intervention?

Question 15.9: The members of the Spanish-speaking group for sex offenders (first described on pages 62-63), challenged the group leader as being unable to help them. Although the leader spoke Spanish fluently, she was Caucasian and not a member of their culture. How could you, as a group leader respond in this situation?

Question 15.10: How has the information in this chapter been similar, as well as different to information from other courses that discuss social diversity?

Question 15.11: Take any scenario that has been offered in this workbook that has struck you as being neglectful of diversity issues. How would you address such issues in the scenario you have chosen?

SUMMARY

Social work has a traditional commitment to helping vulnerable and oppressed populations. Knowledge of diverse groups you are working with is important, as is how to make culturally sensitive adaptations to existing curricula. However, this knowledge should not blind you to the uniqueness of the individuals participating in group interventions. Further, in a world that is becoming increasingly diverse, it may become impossible to know in sufficient depth about a particular social group you will be seeing, particularly when there are members from many diverse groups in your practice settings. Asking strengths-based questions will help you be open to people's perspectives and experiences so that you will be in a better position to help them. In keeping with the focus of this workbook, offering strengths-based approaches will respect and empower people members from diverse groups, as well as all those involved in your group services.

Appendix I: Additional Resources

AFTER-SCHOOL PROGRAMS

After-school programs for youth http://www.casel.org/downloads/ASP-Full.pdf

ANGER MANAGEMENT

Adults

Anger Management for Substance Abuse and Mental Health Clients: A Cognitive Behavioral Therapy Manual: http://kap.samhsa.gov/products/manuals/pdfs/anger1.pdf.

Youth

Jahnke, K. (April, 1998). Anger management programs for children and teens: A review of eleven anger management programs. Paper presented at the Annual Meeting of the National Association of School Psychologists. Retrieved on July 10, 2007 from http://www.eric.ed.gov/ERICDocs/data/ericdocs2sql/content_storage_01/0000019b/80/15/95/e5.pdf

ANXIETY

Child

Hayward, C., Varady, S., Albano, A. M., Thieneman, M., Henderson, L., & Schatzberg, A. F. (2000). Cognitive behavioral group therapy for female socially phobic adolescents: Results of a pilot study. *Journal of the American Academy of Child and Adolescent Psychiatry, 39,* 721–726.

Kendall, P. C. (1990). *Coping Cat workbook.* Ardmore, PA: Workbook. (has been tested in individual, group, and family formats)

Kendall, P. C., Kane, M., Howard, B., & Siqueland, L. (1990). *Cognitive-behavioral treatment of anxious children: Treatment manual.* (Available from P. C. Kendall, Department of Psychology, Temple University, Philadelphia, PA 19122). (has been tested in individual, group, and family formats)

March, J. S., & Mulle, K. (1998). *OCD in children and adolescents: A cognitive behavioral therapy manual.* New York: Guilford Press.

Applied to groups in Thienemann, M., Martin, J., Cregger, B., Thompson, H., & Dyer-Friedman, J. (2001). Manual-driven group cognitive-behavioral therapy for adolescents with obsessive-compulsive disorder: A pilot study. *Journal of the American Academy of Child & Adolescent Psychiatry, 40,* 1254-1260.

CANCER

Living Beyond Limits: Brief Supportive-Expressive Group Therapy for Women with Primary Breast Cancer at http://

pstlab.stanford.edu/bctreat.html. ($20)

CHILD BEHAVIOR PROBLEMS

Webster-Stratton, C. (1981; revised 2001). *Incredible years parents and children training series.* Retrieved September 2, 2004 from http://www.incredibleyears.com.

COGNITIVE-BEHAVIORAL THERAPY

Cognitive-Behavioral Groups for different problems (Panic Disorder and Agoraphobia, Obsessive-Compulsive Disorder, Social Anxiety Disorder, Depression, Bipolar Disorder, Eating Disorders (Binge Eating Disorder and Bulimia), Substance Abuse, and Schizophrenia)

Bieling, P., McCabe, R., & Antony, M. (2006). Cognitive-behavioral therapy in groups. New York: Guilford Press.

CRIME PREVENTION

Preventing Crime: http://www.ncjrs.gov/pdffiles/171676.pdf (a review of what works [and what doesn't] for preventing criminal behavior; some of the interventions involve groups)

DEPRESSION

Youth

Services for Teens at Risk (STAR) depression in youth and post-suicide intervention http://www.wpic.pitt.edu/research/city/FOR%20CLINICIANS/Manuals.htm

Lewinsohn and Clarke curriculum, Adolescent Coping with Depression Course, available at http://www.kpchr.org/public/acwd/acwd.html.

Adult

Group Therapy Manual for Cognitive-Behavioral Treatment of Depression at http://www.rand.org/pubs/monograph_reports/MR1198.4/. ($25)

A description of the above manualized therapy adapted for African-American women is Kohn, L., Oden, T., Muñoz, R., Robinson, A., & Leavitt, D. (2002). Adapted cognitive behavioral group therapy for depressed low-income African American women. *Community Mental Health Journal, 38,* 497-505.

Miranda, J., Green, B., Krupnick, J., Chung, J., Siddique, J., Belin, T., & Revicki, D. (2006). One-year outcomes of a randomized clinical trial treating depression in low-income minority women. *Journal of Consulting and Clinical Psychology, 74,* 99-111. (adapted from above course to be sensitive to the issues of women with histories of interpersonal trauma).

Appendix I: Additional Resources

Manuals available at http://www.hsrcenter.ucla.edu/research/wecare/index.html.

Muñoz, R.F. (1984). The Depression Prevention Course. Unpublished manuscript, University of California, San Francisco. Retrieved on July 10, 2007 from http://medschool.ucsf.edu/latino/pdf/DPC98pnotes.pdf.

ELDERLY

Gallagher-Thompson, D., Ossinalde, C. & Thompson, L.W. (1996a) *Coping with Caregiving: A Class for Family Caregivers.* Palo Alto, CA: VA Palo Alto Health Care System.

Gallagher-Thompson, D., Ossinalde, C. & Thompson, L.W. (1996b) *Como Mantener Su Bienestar.* Palo Alto, CA: VA Palo Alto Health Care System (Spanish Language manual).

Gallagher-Thompson, D., Rose, J., Florsheim, M., Jacome, P., DelMaestro, S., Peters, L., Gantz, F., Arguello, D., Johnson, C., Mooreland, R.S., Polich, T.M., Chesney, M. & Thompson, L.W. (1992) *Controlling your Frustration: A Class for Caregivers.* Palo Alto, CA: VA Palo Alto Health Care System.

Thompson, L., Gallagher, D. & Lovett, S. (1992) *Increasing Life Satisfaction Class: Leaders' and Participant Manuals.* Palo Alto, CA: Dept of Veterans Affairs Medical Center and Standford University.

For these manuals, please write to: Dr Dolores Gallagher-Thompson, Professor of Research, Department of Psychiatry and Behavioral Sciences, Stanford University School of Medicine, California.

EVIDENCE-BASED RESOURCES

http://www.nrepp.samhsa.gov/help-start.htm

HIV

Holistic Health Recovery Program (HHRP+) for the treatment of drug-addicted individuals with HIV disease at http://info.med.yale.edu/psych/3s/HHRP+_manual.html.

Diffusion of Effective Behavioral Interventions, Group Level Treatments at http://effectiveinterventions.org/go/interventions.

SCHIZOPHRENIA

Bellack, A., Mueser, K., Gingerich, S., & Agresta, J. (2004). *Social skills training for schizophrenia: A step-by-step guide, 2nd ed.* New York: The Guilford Press.

SEXUAL ABUSE AND TRAUMA

ChildrenDeblinger, E., & Heflin, A.H. (1996). *Treating sexually abused children and their non-offending parents: A cognitive-behavioral approach.* Thousand Oaks, CA: Sage. (has been tested in both individual and group formats).

Bonner, B., Walker, C.E., & Berliner, L. (n.d.) Treatment manual for cognitive-behavioral group therapy for children with sexual behavior problems. Retrieved on July 7, 2007 from http://www.ncsby.org/pages/publications/CSBP%20Cognitive-behavioral%20child.pdf.

Adults

Harris, M., & Community Connections Trauma Work Group. (1998). Trauma Recovery and Empowerment: A clinician's guide for working with women in groups. New York: Community Connections. Available at http://www.ccdc1.org/publications.htm.

SUBSTANCE USE DISORDERS

Adults

Counseling for Cocaine Addiction: The Collaborative Cocaine Treatment Study Model at http://www.drugabuse.gov/TXManuals/DCCA/DCCA1.html

Motivational groups for community substance abuse programs at http://www.motivationalinterview.org/news/groupguide.html. ($18)

Psychoeducational group therapy for the dually diagnosed at http://www.psychosocial.com/dualdx/psychoed.html. Anderson, A.J. (2001) Psychoeducational group therapy for the dually diagnosed. *International Journal of Psychosocial Rehabilitation,* 5, 77-78.

Relapse Prevention Group at http://kap.samhsa.gov/products/manuals/matrix/text/ctm_05_rp.doc. and an Early Skills Recovery Group at http://kap.samhsa.gov/products/manuals/matrix/text/ctm_04_ers.doc, both from Matrix Manuals at http://kap.samhsa.gov/products/manuals/matrix/index.htm.

Behavioral Couples Therapy for Alcoholism and Drug Abuse which has been used in a group format by Timothy J. O'Farrell and William Fals-Stewart. Available at http://www.ireta.org/online/ and http://www.addictionandfamily.org.

Youth

Model and promising programs for prevention http://www.colorado.edu/cspv/blueprints/index.html.

VIOLENCE PREVENTION

Model and promising programs (some of which involve groups) http://www.colorado.edu/cspv/blueprints/index.html.

References

Ashley, O., Marseden, M.E., & Brady, T. (2003). Effectiveness of substance abuse treatment programming for women: A review. *American Journal of Drug and Alcohol Abuse, 29,* 19-54.

Association for Specialists in Group Work. (1998). *Best practice guidelines.* Retrieved on January 13, 2008 from **Association for Specialists in Group Work**. Website: www.asgw.org/training_standards.htm

Battle, C., Zlotnick, C., & Najavits, L. (2003). Posttraumatic stress disorder and substance use disorder among incarcerated women. In P. Ouimette & P. Brown (Eds.) *Trauma and substance abuse: Causes consequences, and treatment of comorbid disorders* (pp.209-225). Washington, DC: American Psychological Association.

Beach, S., Sandeen, E., & O'Leary, K. (1990). *Depression in marriage: A model for etiology and treatment.* New York: The Guilford Press.

Beatty, R., Geckle, M., Huggins, J., Kapner, C., Lewis, K., Sandstrom, D. (1999). Gay men, lesbians, and bisexuals. In B. McCrady & E. Epstein (Eds.), *Addictions: A comprehensive guidebook* (pp. 542-551). New York, NY: Oxford University Press.

Berg, I.K. (1994). *Family-based services: A solution-focused approach.* New York: W.W. Norton & Company, Inc.

Berg, I.K., & Miller, S. (1992). *Working with the problem drinker.* New York: W.W. Norton & Company, Inc.

Bertolino, B., & O'Hanlon, B. (2002). *Collaborative, competency-based counseling and therapy.* Boston: Allyn & Bacon.

Bieling, P., McCabe, R., & Antony, M. (2006). *Cognitive-behavioral therapy in groups.* New York: The Guilford Press.

Brown, L. (2006). The neglect of lesbian, gay, bisexual, and transgendered clients. In J.C. Norcross, L.E. Beutler, & R.F. Levant (Eds.), *Evidence-based practices in mental health: Debate and dialogue on the fundamental questions* (pp. 346-352). Washington, DC: American Psychological Association.

Cade, B., & O'Hanlon, W.H. (1993). *A brief guide to brief therapy.* New York: W.W. Norton & Company, Inc.

Carroll, K. (1998). *A cognitive-behavioral approach: Treating cocaine addiction.* Retrieved on January 17, 2008 from the National Institute on Drug Abuse. Website:http://www.drugabuse.gov/TXManuals/CBT/CBT1.html.

Christensen, A., Wheeler, J., & Jacobsen, N. (2007). Couple distress. In D.H. Barlow (Ed.), *Clinical Handbook of Psychological Disorders: A Step-by-Step Treatment Manual, 4th edition.* New York, NY: The Guilford Press.

Cohen, J. (1988). *Statistical power analysis for behavioral sciences, 2nd edition.* Hillsdale, NY: Lawrence Earlbaum Associates.

Connors, G., Donovan, D., & DiClemente, C. (2001). *Substance abuse treatment and stages of change: Selecting and planning interventions.* New York: The Guilford Press

Corcoran, J. (2000). *Evidence-based social work practice with families: A lifespan approach.* New York: Springer Publishing.

Corcoran, J. (2003). *Clinical applications of evidence-based family intervention.* New York: Oxford University Press.

Corcoran, J. (2004). *Building strengths and skills: A collaborative approach to working with clients.* New York: Oxford University Press.

Corcoran, J. (2006). *Cognitive-behavioral methods for social workers: A workbook.* Boston: Allyn & Bacon.

Corcoran, J., & Walsh, J. (2006). *Clinical assessment and diagnosis in social work practice.* New York: Oxford University Publishing.

Corey, G. (2008). *Theory and practice of group counseling, 7th edition.* Pacific Grove, CA: Brooks Cole.

Corey, G., Corey, M.S., Callanan, P., Russell, J.M. (2008). *Group techniques, 2nd ed.* Pacific Grove, CA: Brooks Cole.

Corey, M.S., & Corey, G. (2006). *Groups: Process and practice, 7th ed.* Pacific Grove, CA: Brooks Cole.

Council on Social Work Education. (2004). *Educational policy and accreditation standards.* Alexandria, VA: Author.

Deblinger, E. & Heflin, A.H. (1996). *Treating sexually abused children and their nonoffending parents: A cognitive-behavioral approach.* Thousand Oaks, CA: Sage.

DeJong, P., & Berg, I.K. (2002). *Interviewing for solutions,* 2nd ed. Pacific Grove, CA: Brooks Cole.

De Jong, P., Berg, I. K., Kleiner, F. S., & Mamiya, C. J. (2008). *Interviewing for Solutions,* 3rd ed. Pacific Grove, CA: Brooks/Cole.

De Shazer, S. (1994). *Words were originally magic.* New York: Norton.

De Shazer, S., Berg, I.K., Lipchick, E., Nunnally, E., Molnar, A., Gingerich, W., & Weiner-Davis, M. (1986). Brief therapy: Focused solution development. *Family Process, 25,* 207-221.

D'Zurilla, T.J., & Nezu, A.M. (1999). *Problem-solving therapy: A social competence approach to clinical intervention,* 2nd ed. New York: Springer.

Early, T. & Newsome, S. (2005) in J. Corcoran, *Building strengths and skills: A collaborative approach to working with clients* (pp. 359-393). New York, NY: Oxford University Press.

Family Violence Prevention Fund. (2008). Power and control tactics used against immigrant women. Retrieved on January 17, 2008 from Family Violence Prevention Fund. Website:http://www.endabuse.org/programs/display.php3?DocID=111.

References

Gansle, K. (2005). The effectiveness of school-based anger interventions and programs: A meta-analysis. *Journal of School Psychology, 43,* 321-341.

Helgeson, V. S., Reynolds, K. A., & Tomich, P. L.(2006). A meta-analytic review of benefit finding and growth. *Journal of Consulting and Clinical Psychology, 74*(5), 797-816.

Henkel, K. E., Dovidio, J.F., & Gaertner, S. L. (2006). Institutional discrimination, individual racism, and Hurricane Katrina. *Analysis of Social Issues and Public Policy 6*(1), 99-124.

Hepworth, D.H., Rooney, R., Rooney, G., Strom-Gottfried, K., & Larsen, J. (2006). *Direct social work practice: Theory & skills* , 7th ed. Belmont, CA: Brooks/Cole.

Kessler, R.C., Mikelson, K.D., & Williams, D.R. (1999). The prevalence, distribution, and mental health correlates to perceived discrimination in the United States. *Journal of Health and Social Behavior, 40*(3), 208-231.

Kohn, L., Oden, T., & Muñoz, R. (2002). Adapted cognitive behavioral group therapy for depressed low-income African American women. *Community Mental Health Journal, 38*(6), 497-504.

Kolko, D.J. & Wenson, C.C. (2002). *Assessing and treating physically abused children and their families: A cognitive-behavioral approach.* Thousand Oaks, CA: Sage.

Levant, R., & Silverstein, L. (2006). Gender is neglected by both evidence-based practices and treatment as usual. In J.C. Norcross, L.E. Beutler, & R.F. Levant (Eds.), *Evidence-based practices in mental health: Debate and dialogue on the fundamental questions* (pp. 338-345). Washington, DC: American Psychological Association.

Linehan, M. M. (1993). *Cognitive behavioral treatment of borderline clients.* New York: The Guilford Press.

Lundahl, B., Risser, H., & Lovejoy, M.C. (2006). A meta-analysis of parent training: Moderators and follow-up effects. *Clinical psychology Review, 26*(1), 86-104.

Malouff, J., Thorsteinsson, Einar B., Schutte, Nicola S. (2007). The efficacy of problem solving therapy in reducing mental and physical health problems: A meta-analysis. *Clinical psychology review, 27*(1), 46-57.

Miller, W., & Rollnick, S. (2002). *Motivational interviewing: Preparing people to change addictive behavior, 2nd edition.* New York: The Guilford Press.

Miranda, J., Bernal, G., Lau, A., Kohn, L., Hwang, W., & LaFromboise, T. (2005). State of the science on psychosocial interventions for ethnic minorities. *Annual Review of Clinical Psychology, 1,* 113–142.

Miranda, J., Green, B. L., Krupnick, J. L., Chung, J., Siddique, J., Belin, T., & Revicki, D. A. (2007). One-year outcomes of a randomized clinical trail treating depression in low-income minority women. *Journal of Consulting and Clinical Psychology, 74*(1), 99-111.

Muñoz, R.F. (1984). *The depression prevention course.* Retrieved April 15, 2008, from University of California, San Francisco. Website: http://www.medschool.ucsf.edu/latino/pdf/DPC98pnotes.pdf.

Muñoz, R. F., & Mendelson, T. (2005). Toward evidence-based interventions for diverse populations: The San Francisco General Hospital prevention and treatment manuals. *Journal of Consulting and Clinical Psychology, 73*(5), 790-799.

Morris, S., Alexander, J., & Waldron, H. (1988). Functional family therapy. In I.R. Falloon (Ed.), *Handbook of behavioral family therapy.* New York: The Guilford Press.

Moyers, T., Rollnick, S. (2002). A motivational interviewing perspective on resistance in psychotherapy. *JCLP/In Session: Psychotherapy in Practice 58,* 185-193.

Murphy, J. (1997). *Solution-focused counseling in middle and high schools.* Alexandria, VA: American Counseling Association.

National Association of Social Workers. (1999). *Code of ethics.* Alexandria, VA: Author.

Olkin, R., & Taliaferro, G. (2006). Evidence-based practices have ignored people with disabilities. In J.C. Norcross, L.E. Beutler, & R.F. Levant (Eds.), *Evidence-based practices in mental health: Debate and dialogue on the fundamental questions* (pp. 353-358). Washington, DC: American Psychological Association.

O'Hanlon, W.H., & Weiner-Davis, M. (1989). *In search of solutions: A new direction in psychotherapy.* New York: W.W. Norton & Company, Inc.

Petticrew, M., & Roberts, H. (2006). *Systematic reviews in the social sciences: A practical guide.* Oxford, UK: Blackwell Publishing, Ltd.

Prochaska, J., & Norcross, J. (1994). *Systems of psychotherapy: A transtheoretical analysis, 3rd ed.* Pacific Grove, CA: Brooks Cole.

Project MATCH Research group. (1997). Matching alcoholism treatments to client heterogeneity: Project MATCH post treatment drinking outcomes. *Journal of Studies on Alcohol, 58,* 7-29.

Project MATCH research group. (1998). Matching alcoholism treatments to client heterogeneity: Project MATCH three-year drinking outcomes. *Alcoholism: Clinical & Experimental Research, 22,* 1300-1311.

Reid, K.., (1997). *Social work practice with groups: A clinical perspective, 2nd ed.* Pacific Grove, CA: Brooks Cole.

Rooney, R., & Chovanec, M. (2004).m Involuntary groups. In C. D. Garvin, L. M. Gutierrez & M. J. Galinsky (Eds.), *Handbook of social work in groups* (pp. 212-226). New York, NY: The Guilford Press.

Rose, S. (2004). Cognitive behavioral group work. In C.D. Garvin, L.M. Gutierrez, & M.J. Galinsky (Eds.), *Handbook of social work in groups* (pp.111-135). New York, NY: The Guilford Press.

Steinberg, L. (2001). We know some things: Parent-adolescent relationships in retrospect and prospect. *Journal of Research on Adolescence, 11*(1), 1-19.

Sue, S., & Zane, N. (2006). Ethnic minority populations have been neglected by evidence-based practices. In J.C. Norcross, L.E. Beutler, & R.F. Levant (Eds.), *Evidence-based practices in mental health: Debate and dialogue on the fundamental questions* (pp. 329-337). Washington, DC: American Psychological Association.

Toseland, R. W., & Rivas, R. F. (2009). *An introduction to group work practice*, 6th ed. Boston: Allyn & Bacon.

U.S. Department of Health and Human Services. (2001). *Culture, race, and ethnicity: A supplement to mental health: A report of the surgeon general*. Retrieved 2007, from the United States Department of Health & Human Services. Website: http://www.surgeongeneral.gov/library/mentalhealth/cre/.

Webster-Stratton, C., & Herbert, M. (1993). What really happens in parent training? *Behavior Modification, 17*, 407-457.

Whaley, A., & Davis, K. (2007). Cultural competences and evidence-based practice in mental health services: A complementary perspective. *American Psychologist, 62*(6), 563-574.

Wilson, S. J., Lipsey, M. W., & Soydan, H. (2003). Are mainstream programs for juvenile delinquency less effective with minority than majority youth? A meta-analysis of outcomes research. *Research on Social Work Practice, 13*, 3-26.

Wolfe, V.V. (2006). Child sexual abuse. In E.J. Mash and R. Barkley (Eds.), *Treatment of Childhood Disorders, 3rd edition*. New York, Ny: The Guilford Press.

Yalom, I. (1985). *The theory and practice of group psychotherapy*. New York, Basic Books.

Yalom, I. (1995). *The theory and practice of group psychotherapy, 4th edition*. New York, Basic Books.

Yalom, I. (2005). *The theory and practice of group psychotherapy, 5th edition*. New York, Basic Books.

Index

Index

Index

NOTES